Where Did Pluto Go?

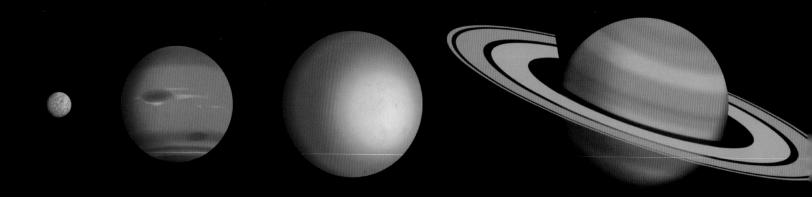

Where Did Pluto Go?

A Beginner's Guide to Understanding the "*New* Solar System"

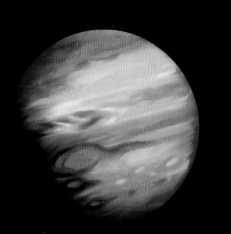
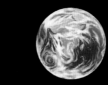

Paul
Sutherland

Foreword by
Neil deGrasse Tyson,
Director of the Hayden
Planetarium

Reader's Digest

The Reader's Digest
Association, Inc.
Pleasantville, NY/
Montreal/Sydney/
Singapore

A READER'S DIGEST BOOK

This edition published by The Reader's Digest Association, Inc.,
by arrangement with Ivy Press

This book was conceived, designed, and produced by
Ivy Press
The Old Candlemakers
West Street, Lewes,
East Sussex BN7 2NZ, U.K.

FOR IVY PRESS
Creative Director Peter Bridgewater
Publisher Jason Hook
Editorial Director Caroline Earle
Art Director Clare Harris
Senior Project Editor Dominique Page
Project Manager Simon Smith
Consultant Editor Iwan Williams, Professor of Mathematics and Astronomy,
Queen Mary, University of London
Designer Glyn Bridgewater
Picture Research Nick Pearson
Concept Design Andrew Milne
Illustrations Greg Smye-Rumsby
Gatefold illustration Lynn Hatzius
Planisphere artwork & design Wil Tirion

FOR READER'S DIGEST
U.S. Project Editor Kimberly Casey
Copy Editor Barbara McIntosh Webb
Canadian Project Editor Pamela Johnson
Australian Project Editor Annette Carter
Senior Art Director George McKeon
Executive Editor, Trade Publishing Dolores York
Associate Publisher Rosanne McManus
President and Publisher, Trade Publishing Harold Clarke

Library of Congress Cataloging in Publication Data:

Sutherland, Paul Graham, 1952-
 Where did Pluto go? : a beginner's guide to understanding the new solar system / Paul
Sutherland.
  p. cm.
 Includes index.
 ISBN 978-0-7621-0977-7
 1. Solar system. 2. Planets. 3. Pluto (Dwarf planet) I. Title.
 QB501.S88 2009
 523.2--dc22

       2008037547

We are committed to both the quality of our products and the service we provide to our
customers. We value your comments, so please feel free to contact us.

The Reader's Digest Association, Inc.
Adult Trade Publishing
Reader's Digest Road
Pleasantville, NY 10570-7000

For more Reader's Digest products and information, visit our website:
    www.rd.com (in the United States)
    www.readersdigest.ca (in Canada)
    www.readersdigest.com.au (in Australia)
    www.readersdigest.com.nz (in New Zealand)
    www.rdasia.com (in Asia)

Printed in China

1 3 5 7 9 10 8 6 4 2

DEDICATION
To my parents, who set me on the road to the stars.

CONTENTS

FOREWORD

Until the mid-twentieth century, planets didn't offer much to talk about. One could track their ever-changing location and brightness on the sky. One could ask how many moons any one of them might have. Or one could venture a guess at what conditions might prevail on their surfaces or within their atmospheres. Under those states of profound yet innocent ignorance, who could blame anyone at the time for thinking that the number of planets and their often memorized sequence from the Sun was a useful display of cosmic knowledge?

As years went by, telescopes got bigger and better, while some became space borne. And NASA began to launch probes to the planets, the moons, the asteroids, and the comets. Many were flybys. Some went into orbit. Others landed and stayed put. Still others landed and then roved. And in the case of Earth's Moon, NASA sent people. Over this time, our knowledge of all that orbits the Sun grew (and continues to grow) exponentially.

By the 1960s we learned that Mars has the largest volcano in the solar system and bears signs of running water from its past—dried riverbeds, floodplains, river deltas. By the 1970s and 1980s, we learned that Saturn was not the only planet with rings. Jupiter, Uranus, and Neptune wear them, too. We also learned that storm systems and ongoing atmospheric chemistry on these gas giants are far more complex than anybody had previously imagined.

As fascinating as the planets had become, in many cases people talked more about planet moons than they did about the planets themselves. Previously amounting to not much

An asteroid crashing into Earth. Collisions were more common in the early solar system. The Moon may have formed when a world the size of Mars struck Earth.

more than orbiting points of light, the larger moons became worlds unto themselves. One with hot volcanoes. Another with ice volcanoes. One with subsurface oceans of water. Another laced with rivers and lakes of liquid methane. And as our knowledge of their sizes became more accurate, we would soon learn that "planet" Pluto was smaller than seven of them—Earth's Moon included.

Meanwhile, the number of cataloged asteroids grew by a factor of 100, and, during the 1990s, a new class of objects was discovered orbiting the Sun in Plutoland—countless thousands of large, icy comets populating a huge swath of real estate beyond the orbit of Neptune.

In the face of all this richness and diversity in our cosmic backyard, to boast that you know how many planets there are and to value that information above all begins to ring hollow.

So the time is now. The time has come to update all those who thought they were done in grade school, after they finished learning "**M**y **V**ery **E**ducated **M**other **J**ust **S**erved **U**s **N**ine **P**izzas" to aid their memory of the nine planets in order from the Sun.

And if you are a big fan of Pluto, not to worry. Yes, he's fallen on hard times, losing the full planetary status he enjoyed in the twentieth century. But, in spite of this book's title, Pluto is surely happier now. What was once the puniest planet is now one of the largest of a new class of objects in a brand-new region of the solar system populated with the icy brethren that Pluto always wanted and now has in abundance.

Welcome to the new solar system.

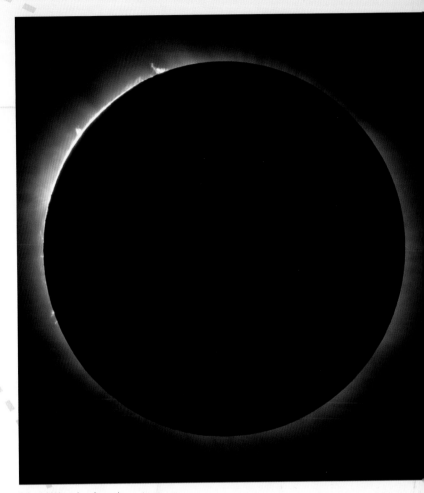

Celestial hide-and-seek reveals prominences and the solar atmosphere in a total eclipse of the Sun in March 2006.

NEIL deGRASSE TYSON
DIRECTOR OF THE HAYDEN PLANETARIUM, NYC

INTRODUCTION

In the early years of the new millennium, our solar system underwent a major upheaval. This was not a result of any dramatic physical event but rather a simple decision that robbed one of the occupants of its status as a planet.

Pluto, which had been the last of nine planets to be discovered in the Sun's family, was unceremoniously demoted to the lesser grade of "dwarf planet," as astronomers struggled to come up with a new definition of what is and isn't a planet. In August 2006 the International Astronomical Union issued those historic new guidelines, causing an uproar among scientists and the public alike, many of whom had learned the order of the planets in childhood by remembering a mnemonic phrase like My Very Educated Mother Just Served Us Nine Pizzas. They now had to wonder: Where did Pluto go?

Some regarded this decision as political interference; others welcomed the debate. But this was really nothing new since change has been the order of things since we first raised our eyes to look at the stars. Much of this change has been due to real happenings over the billions of years since the solar system formed; other changes have come about as a result of our increasing knowledge, thanks to the development of telescopes and space probes. And, as with poor Pluto, some changes are due to a shift in ideas.

"All truths are easy to understand once they are discovered; the point is to discover them."

—GALILEO GALILEI

WHAT WE KNEW THEN

The earliest sky-watchers recognized five planets—Mercury, Venus, Mars, Jupiter, and Saturn—plus the Sun and Moon. Three more planets—Uranus, Neptune, and Pluto—were discovered in the eighteenth, nineteenth, and twentieth centuries, respectively. Together with Earth these brought the total number of known planets to nine.

WHAT WE THINK WE KNOW NOW

The solar system is a cosmic zoo made up of a variety of different inhabitants. Planets can be very different from one another, and they are accompanied by other members of the Sun's family—moons, comets, and asteroids, for example—whose nature we are only just beginning to understand. We are also learning that our solar system is by no means unique.

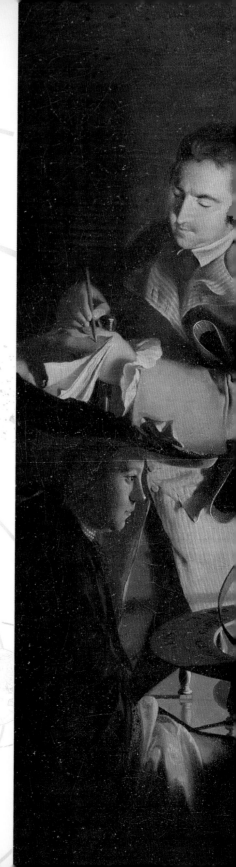

Children watch in wonder as a philosopher demonstrates the movement of the planets with an orrery in this painting by Joseph Wright of Derby, circa 1768.

CHAPTER ONE

MEET THE NEIGHBORS

Early humans had no concept of a solar system or universe. The Sun, Moon, planets, and stars were simply strange lights that could be seen to move above the flat land that they inhabited. There was no idea that we were part of a family of worlds. The first wise men to study the stars were not astronomers, but priests or astrologers interested in the significance of heavenly events rather than their true physical nature. From ancient stone circles or temples built to the gods, they regarded the planets as indicators of our fate. If two planets came close together in a conjunction, that was a powerful sign. Bright comets or eclipses of the Sun and Moon were portents of doom.

Today, with the benefit of the knowledge and wisdom accumulated over centuries, it is easy to scorn the old thinking. It seems blindingly obvious that Earth is spherical, journeys around the Sun, and has celestial neighbors. But we don't feel Earth moving, it doesn't appear to be a sphere, and it in no way resembles those bright dots in the sky. Our judgment comes with the benefit of hindsight.

"I don't believe in astrology; I'm a Sagittarius, and we're skeptical."

—ARTHUR C. CLARKE

WHAT WE KNEW THEN

Early civilizations in China, India, and Greece believed that a flat Earth was surrounded by or floating on a vast ocean. Greek philosopher Anaximander, who lived in the sixth century B.C., imagined that the stars were a view of an inferno through holes in a protective shield that was the sky. Others thought the Sun was carried from west to east by ferryboat through an underground river every night.

WHAT WE THINK WE KNOW NOW

Astrology eventually gave way to astronomy, and science replaced superstition. Today's temples to the stars are observatories, supported by telescopes in space and probes touring the solar system. Their findings show that while the planets may not hold any mystical powers, they are no less fascinating.

Swirling gas and dust begin to collect to form planets around a newly born Sun in the early days of the solar system.

A CELESTIAL JIGSAW

Stars are so far away that their positions appear hardly to change over thousands of years. Ancient man-made patterns formed from the brightest stars became identified with heroes, animals, or mythical beasts. More contemporary designs—such as a microscope, a telescope, and a ship—were created from stars not visible in the northern hemisphere when first seen by European explorers visiting southern lands, thus completing the celestial picture jigsaw.

An astrological representation of the signs of the zodiac. Though astrology was once inextricably linked with astronomy, today it is regarded as a pseudoscience.

PICTURES IN THE SKY

Different civilizations found different pictures in the stars, but today the world recognizes 88 constellations based on an original list compiled by Ptolemy in his famous work the *Almagest* circa A.D. 150. Ptolemy included only 48 in his collection because he could only cover the sky visible throughout the year from Greece, but others have been added over time. The brighter stars are known by the names awarded by ancient civilizations. They were also cataloged by the seventeenth-century German astronomer Johann Bayer, using a Greek letter plus a Latin indicator of the constellation in which they lay. Thus Betelgeuse in Orion is also called Alpha Orionis. Newer catalogs list fainter stars.

The stars that make up Orion, one of the most famous constellations in the sky, though not part of the zodiac.

SIGNS OF THE ZODIAC

The word *planet* comes from the ancient Greek for "wanderer". Early sky-watchers noticed that the planets' movements followed a band of the sky that passed through 12 constellations, which they called the zodiac. The Sun appears to traverse this band along a path called the ecliptic. The 12 traditional signs are: Aries (the Ram), Taurus (the Bull), Gemini (the Twins), Cancer (the Crab), Leo (the Lion), Virgo (the Virgin), Libra (the Scales), Scorpius (the Scorpion), Sagittarius (the Archer), Capricorn (the Sea-Goat), Aquarius (the Water-Bearer), and Pisces (the Fish).

THE 13TH SIGN

Individual constellations might have been distinct, but they used to have rather vague boundaries. That changed when each was allocated a strict region of the sky by the International Astronomical Union (IAU) in 1930. This new precision makes it quite clear that the zodiac has a 13th constellation within it—Ophiuchus (the Healer)—though, curiously, astrologers fail to acknowledge its existence. Perhaps the addition of a sign to the zodiac seems as unthinkable to some as the removal of a planet from the solar system! The southern region of Ophiuchus is crossed by the ecliptic and is therefore home to the Sun in the first weeks of December. You can follow the path of the ecliptic on your planisphere (*see pages 148–9*).

An eighteenth-century star chart that depicts the constellations of the northern and southern skies as a variety of creatures and objects.

DEGREES OF SUCCESS

From their records of the changing heavens, the ancients reckoned the length of a year as being 360 days—only a few days short of the exact duration. And that is why, 5,000 years ago, the circle was divided into 360 units, giving us the degree measurement that mathematicians still use to this day. The number 60 was also seen as special by the Sumerians and later the Babylonians, which explains why degrees and hours are subdivided into 60 minutes and again into 60 seconds.

WHAT WE KNEW THEN

Early man realized that the star patterns occupied different parts of the heavens at different times but in a regular cycle. There was also a rhythmic north–south pattern to the Sun's movements. The seasons were identified, and farmers learned from them to time when to sow seeds or plant crops.

WHAT WE THINK WE KNOW NOW

Today we know that the planets and the Moon all appear to follow similar paths in the heavens because their orbits around the Sun are roughly level with one another. The zodiacal constellations are simply where the planes of those orbits intersect with the starry background.

SPHERES OF INFLUENCE

Early Greek sky-watchers explained the motions of the Sun, Moon, and planets by imagining they were fixed to a number of invisible, concentric spheres. This system put Earth firmly at the center of events, followed by the Moon, Mercury, Venus, the Sun, Mars, Jupiter, and Saturn. Stars were located in the outermost rotating sphere.

The early astronomer and mathematician Ptolemy measures the elevation of the Moon with the aid of an instrument called a quadrant.

WHAT WE KNEW THEN

As the planets blaze their trails across the sky, they can be seen to change direction abruptly at certain times. Mars, Jupiter, and Saturn, for example, follow peculiar loops and run backward against the stars for a few weeks. Since he believed the planets were orbiting Earth, Ptolemy had to produce contrived solutions where the planets made little circular motions, called epicycles, during those orbits.

THE CELESTIAL SPHERE

Today we still imagine the stars as if they were fixed to the inside of a dome like a natural planetarium. This extends right around our planet and is known as the celestial sphere. Viewed from within, we can describe their positions in the sky using a similar method to that for locations on Earth. The celestial equivalents of longitude and latitude are termed *right ascension* (RA) and *declination* (dec). The path of the Sun and planets—the ecliptic—is tilted to the criss-cross grid of RA and dec on the celestial sphere because Earth's axis is tilted by 23.5 degrees to the plane of its orbit.

MISSING MINUTES

The celestial sphere appears to rotate once every 23 hours 56 minutes when measured by the stars—though, of course, it is Earth that is really turning—and this is termed a sidereal day. The solar day we use is 4 minutes longer because of our motion around the Sun, which makes it appear to travel eastward against the starry backdrop. The planisphere with this book maps the area of the celestial sphere that is visible from your part of Earth from hour to hour and night to night (*see pages 148–9*).

The celestial sphere. This demonstrates how the stars appear to be attached to a celestial sphere around Earth. Our axis points toward the north star and the orange line marks the ecliptic.

PLANETARY MOVEMENTS

The English composer Gustav Holst (1874–1934) wrote some real "music of the spheres" in the early twentieth century in the form of his orchestra suite *The Planets* (1914–16). The work is notable for the omission of a movement dedicated to Pluto, which had not then been discovered, and so is actually now in tune with the recent redefining of the solar system.

"Now it is quite clear to me that there are no solid spheres in the heavens, and those that have been devised exist only in the imagination."

—TYCHO BRAHE, SIXTEENTH-CENTURY DANISH ASTRONOMER

A CROSSING POINT

Over time Earth's axis performs a little wobble. This effect, called the precession of the equinoxes, shifts, in cycles of 25,800 years, the points where the ecliptic and celestial equator intersect on the celestial sphere. It means, for example, that the first point of Aries now lies not in Aries at all but instead in the neighboring constellation of Pisces—something the writers of horoscopes rarely mention. Another result of precession will be that new stars will become polestars as Earth's axis advances to point at different spots in the heavens.

WHAT WE THINK WE KNOW NOW

Today it is clear that the planets have not really altered course. The effect, called retrograde motion, is caused by Earth overtaking the more distant worlds during its own orbit around the Sun. It is rather like the moment we might pass a slower car on a freeway—that vehicle will seem to move backward against the distant horizon, too.

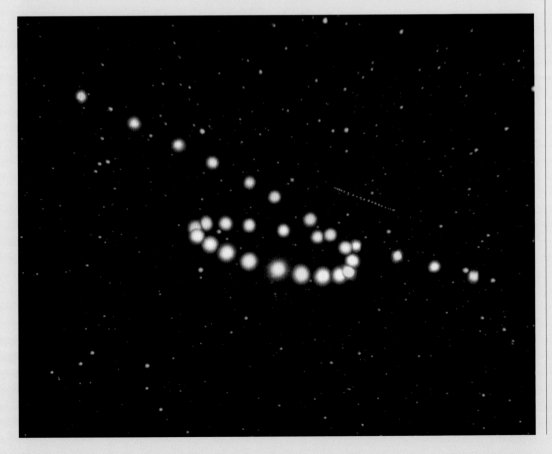

Retrograde motion. A series of photos are superimposed to show the loop described by bright Mars against the starry background. Mars does not really reverse direction; the effect is caused by Earth overtaking Mars in its own orbit around the Sun.

GIANTS OF ASTRONOMY

Our ideas about the solar system and the universe did not change overnight. They evolved over many centuries, as the educated men of the time built on their predecessors' discoveries. Famous early astronomers were astrologers, too. The split between science and pseudoscience did not come about until the advent of what became known as the Age of Reason in the seventeenth century.

The Copernican system. Copernicus's vision of the solar system shifted Earth from the center of the universe to a world orbiting the Sun—a concept that was far more difficult to accept at the time than Pluto's change in status today.

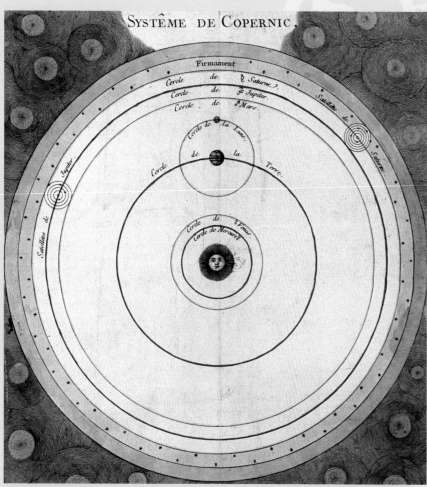

SYSTÊME DE COPERNIC.

AHEAD OF THEIR TIME

A Greek astronomer, Aristarchus, put the Sun at the center of celestial events more than 2,200 years ago, but his ideas were not generally accepted. After the fall of the Roman Empire, scientific endeavor stagnated for centuries in the West, and it was not until the sixteenth century that Polish astronomer Nicolaus Copernicus asserted that Earth was a planet orbiting the Sun. Even then it was such a revolutionary idea that Copernicus published his belief only shortly before his death in 1543.

UNDERSTANDING ORBITS

A sixteenth-century Danish nobleman, Tycho Brahe, took a step backward by reviving the idea that the planets orbited the Sun but that the Sun and Moon revolved around Earth. Despite this, and without the benefit of a telescope, he made a particularly valuable contribution to astronomy by making countless meticulous measurements of the positions of the stars and planets.

Brahe's years of data proved to be a goldmine for the German astronomer Johannes Kepler

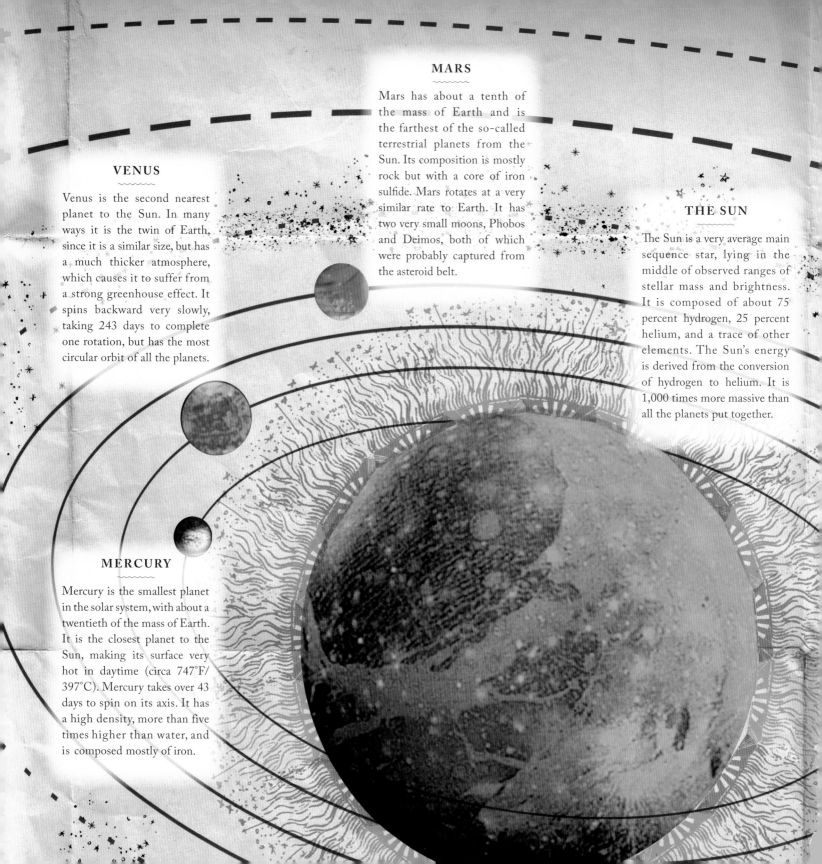

MARS

Mars has about a tenth of the mass of Earth and is the farthest of the so-called terrestrial planets from the Sun. Its composition is mostly rock but with a core of iron sulfide. Mars rotates at a very similar rate to Earth. It has two very small moons, Phobos and Deimos, both of which were probably captured from the asteroid belt.

VENUS

Venus is the second nearest planet to the Sun. In many ways it is the twin of Earth, since it is a similar size, but has a much thicker atmosphere, which causes it to suffer from a strong greenhouse effect. It spins backward very slowly, taking 243 days to complete one rotation, but has the most circular orbit of all the planets.

THE SUN

The Sun is a very average main sequence star, lying in the middle of observed ranges of stellar mass and brightness. It is composed of about 75 percent hydrogen, 25 percent helium, and a trace of other elements. The Sun's energy is derived from the conversion of hydrogen to helium. It is 1,000 times more massive than all the planets put together.

MERCURY

Mercury is the smallest planet in the solar system, with about a twentieth of the mass of Earth. It is the closest planet to the Sun, making its surface very hot in daytime (circa 747°F/ 397°C). Mercury takes over 43 days to spin on its axis. It has a high density, more than five times higher than water, and is composed mostly of iron.

THE SOLAR SYSTEM

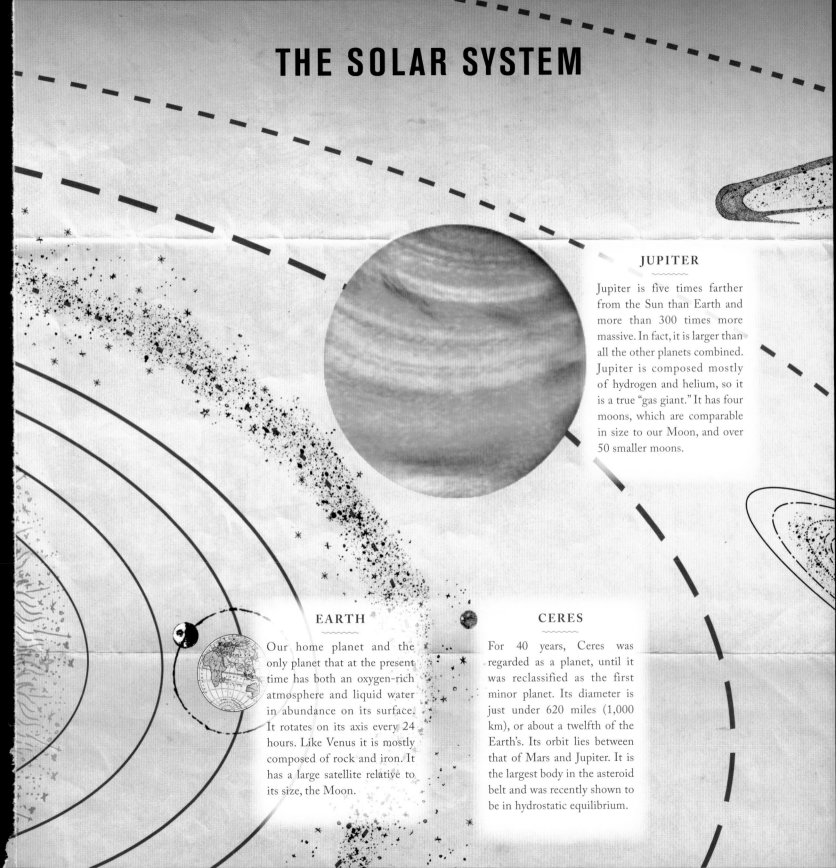

JUPITER

Jupiter is five times farther from the Sun than Earth and more than 300 times more massive. In fact, it is larger than all the other planets combined. Jupiter is composed mostly of hydrogen and helium, so it is a true "gas giant." It has four moons, which are comparable in size to our Moon, and over 50 smaller moons.

EARTH

Our home planet and the only planet that at the present time has both an oxygen-rich atmosphere and liquid water in abundance on its surface. It rotates on its axis every 24 hours. Like Venus it is mostly composed of rock and iron. It has a large satellite relative to its size, the Moon.

CERES

For 40 years, Ceres was regarded as a planet, until it was reclassified as the first minor planet. Its diameter is just under 620 miles (1,000 km), or about a twelfth of the Earth's. Its orbit lies between that of Mars and Jupiter. It is the largest body in the asteroid belt and was recently shown to be in hydrostatic equilibrium.

MAKEMAKE

Makemake is the third largest dwarf planet in the solar system with a diameter three-quarters that of Pluto. It orbits high above the ecliptic, which may explain why it evaded discovery until March 2005. Makemake was classified as a plutoid in July 2008. It has no known satellites.

NEPTUNE

Neptune is now the outermost of the main planets, and it is 30 times farther from the Sun than Earth. It is very similar to Uranus, but slightly smaller, at 14 Earth masses. Neptune has a large moon, Triton, and it also has an important effect on the behavior of objects in the Kuiper Belt.

ERIS

Eris, discovered in 2003, is slightly larger than Pluto. Its average distance from the Sun is nearly 70 times that of Earth but its orbit is so elongated that it crosses the orbits of both Neptune and Pluto. Its inclination of nearly 36 degrees takes it well out of the zodiacal band for most of its orbit.

PLUTO

Pluto has only 0.2 percent of the mass of Earth, and under 20 percent of the Moon's mass. Its average distance from the Sun is nearly 40 times that of Earth, and it orbits the Sun twice for every three orbits of Neptune. It never has a close approach to Neptune despite having an elongated orbit that sometimes takes it inside the Neptunian orbit.

CHARON

Charon is a moon of Pluto. It has a mass of only 2 percent of our Moon, but has the highest mass ratio of moon to parent in the solar system. Uniquely, the center of mass of the Pluto-Charon system is outside Pluto, leading some to claim that this is a "double dwarf planet system" rather than a moon orbiting the parent.

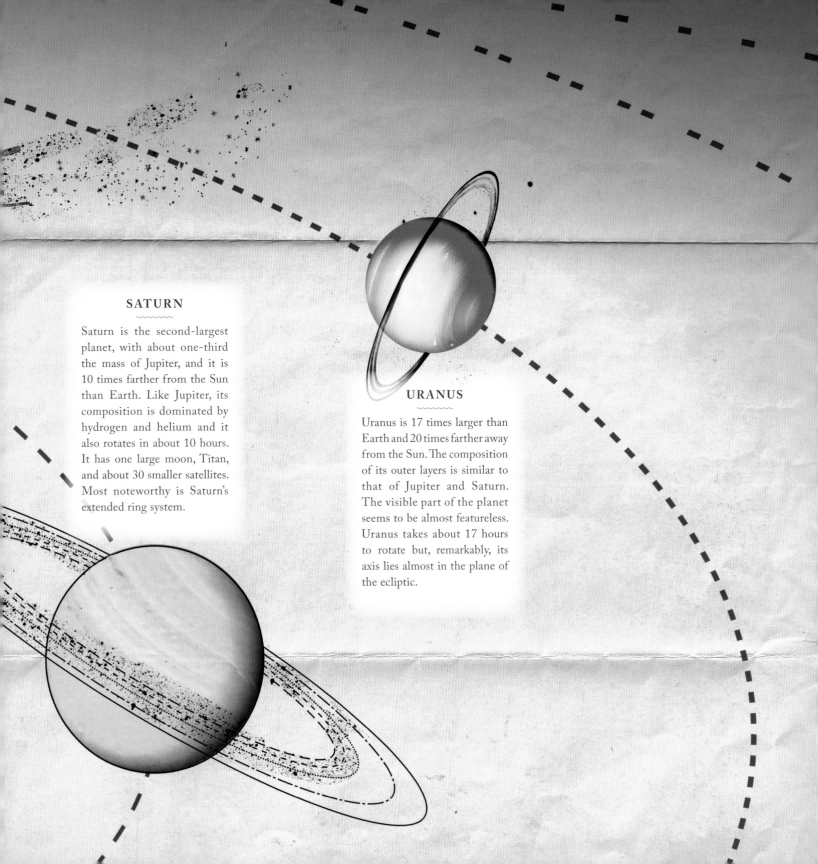

SATURN

Saturn is the second-largest planet, with about one-third the mass of Jupiter, and it is 10 times farther from the Sun than Earth. Like Jupiter, its composition is dominated by hydrogen and helium and it also rotates in about 10 hours. It has one large moon, Titan, and about 30 smaller satellites. Most noteworthy is Saturn's extended ring system.

URANUS

Uranus is 17 times larger than Earth and 20 times farther away from the Sun. The composition of its outer layers is similar to that of Jupiter and Saturn. The visible part of the planet seems to be almost featureless. Uranus takes about 17 hours to rotate but, remarkably, its axis lies almost in the plane of the ecliptic.

(1571–1630). Kepler agreed with Copernicus that the Sun was central, but his real breakthrough was to understand that the planets' orbits are elliptical and not circular. He drew up three laws of planetary motion to explain how the planets moved through space. Kepler deduced that a planet's speed varies in different sections of its orbit, being faster when closer to the Sun. He further proved that the time a planet takes to complete an orbit is dictated by its distance from the Sun. Kepler subscribed to the ancient notion of a cosmic harmony, often called the music of the spheres—though this particular music is silent!

SCOPE FOR CHANGE

Galileo Galilei (1564–1642), a professor of mathematics in Padua, Italy, was among the first to use the newly invented telescope as an astronomical tool. Observations with his powerful "optick tube" refractor revealed the Moon's rugged landscape, lunarlike phases of Venus, four main moons of Jupiter, and dark blemishes on the Sun. He also observed Saturn's rings but wrongly believed he was seeing three worlds oddly joined together. Galileo suffered trial and arrest by the Church for daring to support Copernicus's model that removed Earth from the center of the universe. He was not officially cleared by the Roman Catholic Church until 1983. As was common practice at the time, Galileo protected his discoveries by disguising them as anagrams in Latin until he was ready to publish them.

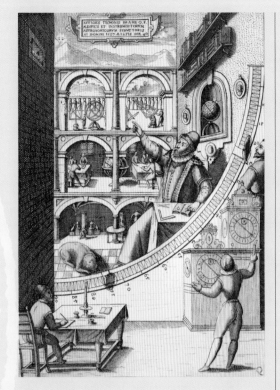

Tycho Brahe regards the heavens amid frenetic activity at his castle observatory on the island of Hven, Denmark.

"*Truth is the daughter of time, and I feel no shame in being her midwife.*"

—JOHANNES KEPLER

THE POWER OF ATTRACTION

English professor Sir Isaac Newton (1643–1727) supplied the final piece of the jigsaw when, allegedly inspired by a falling apple, he identified gravity. He realized that this was the great force that attracted bodies in the universe to one another, keeping planets in their orbits rather than flying off in a straight line. He also invented a new telescope, the Newtonian, which used a mirror instead of a lens to collect light, thus avoiding false-color issues that lenses can introduce by refracting different parts of the spectrum to different points when light passes through them.

BIRTH OF THE SOLAR SYSTEM

Everything in our solar system was produced from a great cloud of dust and gas in space, some of it the remains of dead stars, that happened to collect together. What is more, astronomers now know that the birth of our family of planets was not a unique event.

A disk of dust imaged by the Hubble space telescope around HD 107146—a yellow dwarf star, 88 light years away from Earth—that is much like our Sun but considerably younger.

COSMIC WHIRLPOOL

As early as 1644 the great French thinker René Descartes had contemplated the origin of the planets, suggesting that a whirlpool of matter had turned into the Sun and other bodies. Descartes's concept was similar to our understanding today, though he had no concept of gravity and so no valid explanation of what caused this to occur. In 1755 the philosopher Immanuel Kant was first to suggest that the worlds condensed from an enormous disk of gas and dust. The Marquis de Laplace, a French mathematician, expressed a similar idea in 1809, now known as the Nebular Hypothesis.

VIOLENT INTERACTION

A rival idea for the formation of the solar system, one that endured well into the twentieth century, was that a violent interaction between the Sun and another celestial body had produced the planets. In eighteenth-century France, Georges-Louis Leclerc, Comte de Buffon, proposed that a giant comet had been the cause. Later astronomers suggested instead that the tidal influence of a passing star had drawn the matter out from the Sun that formed into its family of worlds. If this scenario had been correct, it would have meant that the birth of a solar system such as ours was a rare, perhaps unique, event. As it is, the theory has now been dismissed.

INTERSTELLAR INCUBATOR

Today we know that our solar system was originally part of a vast cloud of dust particles and gases—mainly hydrogen, with helium, carbon, nitrogen, and oxygen. A little over 4.6 billion years ago, something as yet unknown triggered a change so that the cloud began to condense into globules, an effect described in the early twentieth century by leading British astronomer Sir James Jeans. The cloud became a cosmic nursery as the globules contracted, heated up, and hatched into stars, one of which became our Sun. The substance of the cloud was probably leftover material from supernova explosions—thus the deaths of old stars gave birth to new ones. As the Sun formed, it became encircled by a wide, flat disk of dust and gas. In the late twentieth century, similar disks—called protoplanetary disks, or proplyds, because astronomers believe that planets will form from them—were detected around other stars. A number were found in the heart of the Orion Nebula, which is known to be a cosmic nursery, and a heat-seeking satellite called the Infrared Astronomical Satellite (IRAS), observing in the infrared part of the spectrum, imaged dusty disks around a number of other stars, including one of the brightest in our night sky, Vega.

COSMIC CONSTRUCTION SITE

Conditions were violent during the birth of the solar system. As the dust and rock swirling around in the cloud collided, it all began to clump together to form larger bodies called planetesimals. These, in turn, grew into protoplanets, which over millions of years built up into the planets we know today.

A CLEAN SWEEP

Dust and gas were blown away by the solar wind, possibly forming the vast clouds of icy fragments that scientists believe lie beyond the known planets. The planets swept their orbits free of smaller rocky bodies, leaving the solar system as the relatively calm place we find in our time.

Cosmic dust. An artist's impression of a very young star encircled by a disk of gas and dust, the raw materials from which rocky planets such as Earth are thought to form.

A FAMILY OF WORLDS

As in any family, the solar system contains an assortment of characters. The four inner planets, including Earth, are rocky worlds. After a zone of smaller rocky asteroids come four siblings that are essentially giant balls of gas. Finally, ex-planet Pluto opens the door to a new realm of mysterious icy bodies from which jaywalking comets regularly flit across the space lanes.

ROCKY AND GASSY WORLDS

The inner worlds of the solar system—Mercury, Venus, Earth, and Mars—are solid because only rocks and metals could endure the intense heat in the inner regions of the protoplanetary disk; gases could not survive and were vaporized. The situation was different in the cooler outer regions, where vast quantities of frozen gases combined with rocky chunks to build the giant planets of Jupiter, Saturn, Uranus, and Neptune.

A DEFINING MOMENT

In 2006 the International Astronomical Union held a meeting in Prague to tighten up the definition of what constitutes a planet. A controversial vote declared it to be a celestial body that was in orbit around the Sun, had sufficient mass to form a fairly spherical shape, and had cleared other debris from the region of its orbit. The meeting introduced a new class of objects called dwarf planets, a category to which Pluto has now been consigned.

The rotation periods of Venus and Uranus are shown as negative figures in the table below because they spin in the opposite direction to the other planets.

Inclination is the amount in degrees that an orbit is tilted from that of Earth.

Eccentricity is a measure of how elliptical the orbit is; that is, how much it deviates from a circle.

A TABLE OF PLANETARY DATA

Planet	Radius at equator (x 1,000 miles / km)	Rotation (days)	Distance from Sun (x 1,000 miles / km)	Orbital period days (years)	Inclination	Eccentricity
Sun	43,185 / 69,500	24.6	—	—	—	—
Mercury	1,516 / 2,440	58.6	35,984 / 57,910	87.97	7	0.21
Venus	3,760 / 6,052	-243	67,232 / 108,200	224.7	3.39	0.01
Earth	3,963 / 6,378	0.99	92,957 / 149,600	365.26	0	0.02
Mars	2,111 / 3,397	1.03	141,635 / 227,940	686.98 (1.88)	1.85	0.09
Jupiter	44,423 / 71,492	0.41	483,632 / 778,330	4332.71 (11.86)	1.31	0.05
Saturn	37,449 / 60,268	0.45	888,188 / 1,429,400	10759.5 (29.46)	2.49	0.06
Uranus	15,882 / 25,559	-0.72	1,783,950 / 2,870,990	30685 (84.01)	0.77	0.05
Neptune	15,389 / 24,766	0.67	2,798,841 / 4,504,300	60190 (164.79)	1.77	0.01

THE MISSING PLANET

In the layout of bodies in the solar system, there is a large gap between Mars and Jupiter where one might instinctively expect another planet to lie. Instead, this zone is inhabited by the asteroid belt, which comprises many millions of rocky fragments that range in size from small rocks to the newly labeled dwarf planet Ceres, which is 590 miles (950 km) in diameter. Astronomers used to wonder whether asteroids were the debris of another planet that had been torn to pieces in a cataclysmic event. However, the current view is that they are fragments that failed to collect together in the first place because of the gravitational influence of Jupiter.

How Earth, the Moon, and dwarf planet Ceres measure up in size when compared to each other.

AN INFERIORITY COMPLEX

Mercury and Venus are the inferior planets—not because there is anything wrong with them, but because they lie *within* Earth's orbit. Worlds beyond our orbit—Mars to Neptune—are, similarly, labeled superior. When an inferior planet passes between Earth and the Sun, it is said to be at inferior conjunction; on the far side it reaches superior conjunction. A superior planet is said to be at opposition when Earth lies between it and the Sun and at conjunction when on the far side of the Sun.

PLANETARY PATTERNS

In 1768 Johann Elert Bode highlighted a curious pattern to the distances of the planets. It showed that if you took the sequence 0, 3, 6, 12, 24, 48, 96, and so on, added 4 to each number, and then divided it by 10, this produced a sequence 0.4, 0.7, 1.0, 1.6, 2.8, 5.2, 10.0, which closely matched the relative distances from the Sun of the seven planets then known. Called Bode's Law, this formula appeared to be confirmed by the later discoveries of Uranus and the dwarf planet Ceres, but it is still unclear whether the pattern has any real scientific value.

Johann Bode, the German astronomer who detected a mathematical pattern in the distances of the planets from the Sun.

"There are more things in heaven and Earth, Horatio, Than are dreamt of in your philosophy."

—WILLIAM SHAKESPEARE, "HAMLET"

CHAPTER TWO

THE SUN

Many civilizations across the world have worshipped the Sun as a deity. Ancient peoples were in awe of its enormous power, of how it provided light and heat, and they were plunged into fear and darkness by its absence. With the illumination of knowledge and reason, we have learned that the Sun is just a typical star, but that does not diminish its life-supporting powers. Astronomically the Sun is important because it is the only star that we are able to study close up. Its light reaches us in just eight and a half minutes. From the next nearest star, Proxima Centauri, it takes a lot longer—four and a half years!

The Sun is a main sequence star, being, at an age of 4.5 billion years, about halfway along the path of a typical star's evolutionary cycle. It is at a relatively stable stage called a yellow dwarf—though this dwarf is big enough to hold a million Earths. In another 5 or 6 billion years it will grow much larger, becoming a red giant that really could increase enough in size to swallow Earth in its orbit. The Sun does not burn like a fire. Rather, it is a nuclear powerhouse, producing energy by converting 4 million tons of hydrogen into helium every second.

"Finally we shall place the Sun himself at the center of the Universe."

—Nicolaus Copernicus

WHAT WE KNEW THEN

William Herschel, who discovered Uranus in 1781, was convinced that the Sun was inhabited by aliens who were protected from the searing heat by layers of clouds. As late as 1951 a German engineer, Godfried Büren, offered a cash prize to anyone who could prove that the Sun was not inhabited. A court ordered him to pay out to a German astronomical society.

WHAT WE THINK WE KNOW NOW

Modern science-fiction writers have continued to write about the possibility of life on the Sun. However, we finally learned what the inside of the Sun is really like from the study of seismological disturbances, or sunquakes. Matched with computer models, they point to a center that burns at an incredible 25 million degrees Fahrenheit (14 million degrees Celsius).

From an imaginary vantage point in the inner solar system, spots can be seen on the Sun as well as hot gas streaming into space.

SUNSPOTS AND THE SURFACE

Before the development of the telescope, dark blotches on the Sun's disk were often big enough to be seen with the naked eye at sunrise or sunset, or through cloud cover, and Chinese records of sunspots go back more than 2,000 years. But because Aristotle deemed heavenly bodies to be perfect, such blemishes tended to be ignored or wrongly explained away as being, for example, the planet Mercury silhouetted against the solar disk.

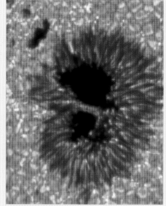

Sunspots. A classic image of a sunspot, with its dark central umbra surrounded by a lighter penumbra. The granulated patterns on the Sun's surface are clearly visible.

A twelfth-century sketch of a giant sunspot from the *Chronicles of John of Worcester.*

SOLAR ACNE

Despite reaching middle age, the Sun often breaks out in spots. Careful observation of sunspots reveals that they have a dark center and a lighter surround, termed the *umbra* and *penumbra*, respectively. Often many times bigger than Earth, these spots are relatively cooler regions that appear dark only by contrast with the rest of the Sun's visible surface, which is called the photosphere.

However, they are in fact really glowing brilliantly at about 7,200°F (4,000°C). Over a solar cycle the general position of spots on the Sun's disk migrates from the poles toward the equator as activity diminishes. When plotted over time on a graph, this effect resembles the wings of a butterfly.

Intricate sketches by Christoph Scheiner, from 1630, of sunspots changing position from day to day as the Sun rotates.

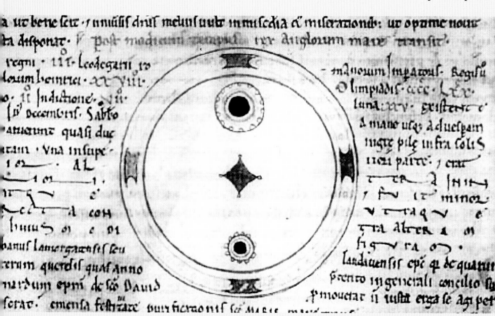

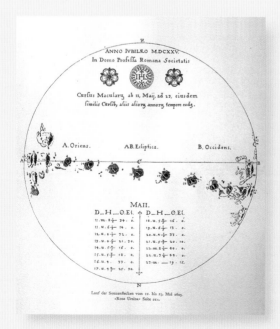

THE SOLAR CYCLE

German pharmacist Heinrich Schwabe was, in the mid-nineteenth century, the first to notice that sunspots appeared more frequently in some years than in others. Rudolf Wolf, of Bern Observatory in Switzerland, confirmed a cycle of activity in the Sun that lasted roughly 11 years. The pattern could be traced through sunspot records stretching back to Galileo's time, though the level of activity varied from cycle to cycle. In particular, few spots were seen in a very quiet spell for a hundred years to 1750. It is termed the Maunder minimum, after the English astronomer Edward Maunder, who, in 1893, first noted their paucity in the records. The northern hemisphere suffered a very prolonged cold spell—known as the Little Ice Age—following the Maunder minimum, leading some scientists to wonder if solar activity might be linked to climate change.

A MAGNETIC PERSONALITY

Pioneering work in studying sunspots was carried out at the world's first dedicated solar observatory at Mount Wilson, California. In 1908 George Ellery Hale discovered from their spectra that they were produced in a powerful magnetic field, like iron filings drawn to a magnet. Further studies showed that the spots tended to appear in pairs with opposite polarities. Most surprisingly, Hale found that the directions of the spots' north–south polarities reversed with a new solar cycle, showing that the 11-year cycle was in fact a 22-year magnetic cycle.

A HEATED HONEYCOMB

The photosphere is not smooth but has a granulated pattern of cells like a honeycomb, which is constantly changing as convection currents carry gas from inside the Sun to the surface at supersonic speeds before it cools and falls again. This constant churning is driven by the Sun's magnetic field, which is now thought to be produced because different layers of the Sun rotate at different speeds. Small bright areas that appear around sunspots but can outlast them are known as plages. Bright streams seen running between the surface granules are called faculae, and they are created where lines of the magnetic field become concentrated.

EYES IN THE SKY

Because our star is dangerously bright, sunspots should only be viewed using a telescope fitted with an appropriate filter or one that projects the Sun's image onto a card. After the invention of the telescope, early observers such as Galileo and England's Thomas Harriot first viewed sunspots using the new technology in about 1610, and Johannes Fabricius and his father, David, recorded several soon afterward, tracking their movement as the Sun turned. Sketches by their German contemporary Christoph Scheiner showed that sunspots changed shape from day to day. His observations also revealed that the spinning Sun must be tilted on its axis. In 1863 the British amateur astronomer Richard Carrington noticed from his observations of sunspots that different parts of the Sun rotate at different speeds. The equatorial region turns approximately once every 25 days, but nearer the poles it takes 35 days to rotate.

George Ellery Hale uses an instrument of his own invention called a spectroheliograph to observe the Sun at Mount Wilson Observatory near Los Angeles, California.

INSIDE THE FURNACE

The Sun is not a solid body but a ball of gases, including a special type sensitive to magnetism, called plasma. The photosphere is just the visible layer rather than the surface. Examining the Sun in other parts of the spectrum reveals different outer regions. The interior of the Sun, once a complete mystery, is finally revealing its secrets, thanks to rippling waves from sunquakes that make it ring, or vibrate, like a bell.

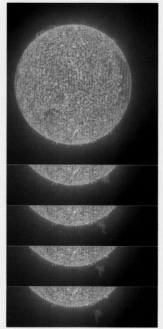

A solar prominence. This sequence of images shows how a solar prominence erupts and changes over a few hours.

THE HEART OF THE SUN

The Sun's core is where its fantastic energy output is produced. It constitutes 20 percent of the diameter of the Sun, and temperatures there are close to 25 million degrees Fahrenheit (14 million degrees Celsius), while its matter is 150 times denser than the water in our oceans. Outside the core is the radiative zone, which extends outward to about 70 percent of the distance to the Sun's visible edge. Beyond this is the convective zone, in which columns of heated material are carried out to the surface where they cool and descend again. Sunlight is born in the core but takes between 10,000 and 170,000 years to reach the surface—then just less than nine seconds to reach Earth. This surprisingly long time spent fighting a path through the Sun is actually quicker than it was once thought, because textbooks used to quote a journey time of up to 50 million years!

This cutaway diagram reveals the different layers found in the Sun. In the nineteenth century, before the nuclear processes that power our home star were understood, it was thought the Sun might be a giant lump of coal. If it had been, it would have burned out in less than 6,000 years.

INSIDE OUR SUN

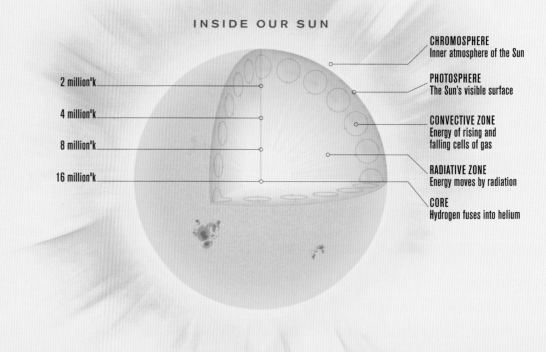

2 million°k

4 million°k

8 million°k

16 million°k

CHROMOSPHERE
Inner atmosphere of the Sun

PHOTOSPHERE
The Sun's visible surface

CONVECTIVE ZONE
Energy of rising and falling cells of gas

RADIATIVE ZONE
Energy moves by radiation

CORE
Hydrogen fuses into helium

THE SUN'S ATMOSPHERE

Above the photosphere, which marks the visible surface, are the layers of the Sun's atmosphere. The *chromosphere* is a region 6,000 miles (10,000 km) deep in which flamelike prominences, spikes, and wisps of hot gas are ejected under high pressure from the photosphere. Prominences can sometimes break away from the surface altogether, and many are big enough to be seen around the edge of a totally eclipsed Sun. Beyond the chromosphere, stretching for millions of miles into space, is the *corona*, which shows itself as a ghostly glow during total eclipses, its shape changing according to the Sun's point in its 11-year cycle. Finally, there is the heliosphere, a stream of charged particles flowing out at supersonic speeds beyond the orbits of all the planets—and Pluto. Strangely, the temperature rises significantly through the atmosphere, from 10,800°F (6,000°C) at the surface through 36,000°F (20,000°C) in the chromosphere to between 3.5 and 5.5 million degrees Fahrenheit (2 and 3 million degrees Celsius) in the corona. Recent studies suggest this is caused by material from the Sun hitting an invisible barrier in the corona and releasing energy.

OTHER ERUPTIONS

In 1859 the amateur astronomers Richard Carrington and Richard Hodgson were the first to observe solar flares, the huge explosions that occur above some active sunspot groups, becoming visible at all wavelengths. Greater eruptions are called coronal mass ejections.

A solar barcode. The German optician Joseph von Fraunhofer demonstrates his spectroscope, which allowed him to discover what the Sun and other stars are made of by breaking light in such a way that its elemental makeup is revealed.

These occur when highly charged plasma is hurled from the Sun into space—a phenomenon known as space weather. Coronal mass ejections are a threat to satellite electronics, power grids, and even astronauts' lives. In fact, the flare seen in 1859 preceded the biggest geomagnetic storm on record, causing telegraph communications to be disrupted and brilliant displays of the northern and southern lights.

THE SPECTROSCOPE

A breakthrough in the study of the Sun—and, indeed, all stars—came in 1814 when a German optician, Joseph von Fraunhofer, invented the spectroscope. This device breaks a beam of light into a rainbow of colors, which appears crossed by a number of dark lines like a cosmic barcode. Called absorption lines, these are the fingerprints of different elements, and astronomers were at last able to deduce from them what the Sun is made of. Fraunhofer recorded 574 of these lines in sunlight and went on to examine some of the brighter stars, revealing them to have their own unique elemental makeup.

"The Sun, with all the planets revolving around it, and depending on it, can still ripen a bunch of grapes as though it had nothing else in the Universe to do."

—GALILEO GALILEI

CHAPTER THREE

EARTH

Because we live on Earth, it is easy to forget that it is a planet like the others. Ours is the third rock from the Sun, a solid world like Mercury and neighbors Mars and Venus. But the link between Earth and other planets was not clear to ancient peoples, who saw a distinct difference between their immediate surroundings and the stars and worlds that filled the heavens. Before educated minds grasped that Earth was round, it was generally thought to be flat.

Of course, Earth is not really quite like other worlds and is, indeed, rather special. It occupies a region of the solar system ideal for life, which has flourished in abundance, creating millions of species of animals, insects, and plants. The region of Earth that contains and supports life is known as the biosphere, which includes the vast oceans that cover 70 percent of the planet—another respect in which Earth is unique. Earth appears as a fragile blue marble from space, decorated with ever-changing swirls of clouds. The lights of major cities, industries, and oil fields blaze on the night side, alerting any passing aliens to our presence.

WHAT WE KNEW THEN

Greek thinker Eratosthenes realized Earth was a sphere and, some time about 200 B.C., set out to measure its circumference. He used the shadow of a stick to work out the height of the noonday sun at different locations in Egypt. From these measurements he calculated a figure that, by luck or by judgment, was remarkably close to the truth.

WHAT WE THINK WE KNOW NOW

Earth is a living world with geological and atmospheric activity that slowly but steadily changes its nature and appearance. Though regions deep in the oceans remain as unexplored as distant planets, many aspects of our world are being studied both on the ground and from space.

"The surface of the Earth is the shore of the cosmic ocean. From it we have learned most of what we know."

—CARL SAGAN

The bright glow from human settlements on the night side of Earth rival the lights of the stars far away in space.

ROCKY III

Despite the fact that we live on it, scientists have barely scratched the surface of the third planet. However, studies of earthquakes and the nature of rocks near the surface, together with calculations of Earth's "weight," have allowed scientists to speculate with some authority on what lies beneath our feet.

THE WEIGHT OF EVIDENCE

It is impossible to weigh Earth on a set of scales. Instead, its gravitational pull combined with its size, orbit, and effects on the Moon and other planets have enabled astronomers to calculate its mass and density. Their results reveal that Earth is the densest of the planets, and its center must be much denser than the surface.

In 1692 Edmond Halley—of comet fame—suggested, in an attempt to explain why it seemed less dense than the Moon, that Earth was hollow. He suggested that inside were two other concentric spheres surrounding a core the size of Mercury. The theory was later taken up by others, such as the American John Cleves Symmes, who in 1818 was convinced that openings into the void would be found at the north and south poles.

JOURNEY TO THE CENTER OF THE EARTH

The solid ground on which we walk is the outer crust of Earth, and it ranges from just 3 miles (5 km) deep at some parts of the ocean floor to 45 miles (70 km) at its thickest point. Below the crust is the mantle, a layer of heated rock 1,795 miles (2,890 km) deep, which is much richer in iron and magnesium than the surface. While still solid, it is flexible like a viscous liquid. Earth has a solid center about 1,500 miles (2,400 km) across and mainly composed of iron, but this core is wrapped in a liquid outer layer that is another 590 miles (960 km) thick. Earth's center may be hotter than the surface of the Sun!

Volcanoes occur at hotspots where rock from the mantle melts and bursts through the

Although we have not drilled down very far, scientific detective work has told us what lies inside Earth.

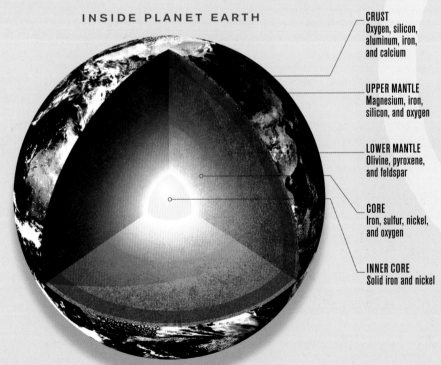

INSIDE PLANET EARTH

CRUST
Oxygen, silicon, aluminum, iron, and calcium

UPPER MANTLE
Magnesium, iron, silicon, and oxygen

LOWER MANTLE
Olivine, pyroxene, and feldspar

CORE
Iron, sulfur, nickel, and oxygen

INNER CORE
Solid iron and nickel

Kilauea, in the Hawaiian Islands, the world's most active volcano, has been pouring out lava continuously since 1983.

crust under pressure. This process, known as volcanism, was blamed by ancient man on angry gods. Greek thinkers, including Plato, believed volcanoes were fed by an underground river of fire that was driven by the wind.

THE DATING GAME

It may seem curious that we are able to calculate the age of Earth, but the secret is locked inside the rocks themselves. Most contain tiny traces of radioactive elements that gradually decay, or break down, into other elements. The rate of decay for each element is fixed, allowing us to tell precisely the rock's age from the state of the elements it contains. This technique was pioneered by English scientist Arthur Holmes who, by 1946, declared that our planet was at least 3 billion years old. Scientists subsequently refined the age to 4.5 billion years.

The figure is a huge advance on that of Irish Archbishop James Ussher who, in 1654, declared the age of Earth to be 6,000 years, a woefully inadequate estimate that was never-theless widely accepted until well into the eighteenth century.

HEALING THE SCARS

Our planet was not spared the cosmic battering by asteroids and comets that left scars on the Moon and planets such as Mercury. But movement of the crust, weathering, and other forces of erosion have wiped away much of the evidence. Ancient craters are still being found, though the signs have faded like old photographs in a drawer.

A BULGING MIDRIFF

Earth is not a perfect sphere: it bulges slightly at the equator because of Its rotation. This difference of around 13 miles (21 km) means that the farthest point from the center of our planet is not the summit of Mount Everest—at 29,028 feet (8,848 m) above sea level—but the peak of the volcano Chimborazo in Ecuador. Chimborazo, though only 20,565 feet (6,268 m) above sea level, is 3,968 miles (6,384.4 km) from Earth's core—1½ miles (nearly 2 km) farther than Everest's summit.

> *"We live on an insignificant planet of a humdrum star lost in a galaxy tucked away in some forgotten corner of a universe."*
> —CARL SAGAN

The Arizona Meteor Crater is a spectacular, mile-wide impact scar created about 50,000 years ago.

EXPLORING OUR PLANET

Humans have been making maps almost from the time we first began to think about our surroundings. The oldest maps surviving today were carved on clay tablets by the Babylonians in around 2300 B.C., and the ancient Greeks and Romans followed, skillfully mapping out the lands that they knew.

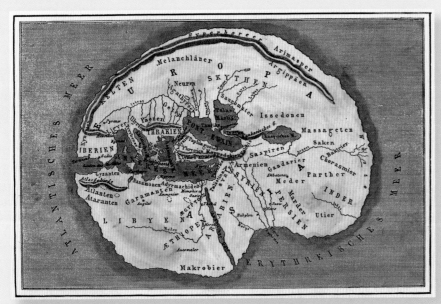

Expanding horizons. This nineteenth-century woodcut depicts the limited world as understood by the Greek historian Herodotus more than 400 years B.C.

CHARTING PROGRESS

The first maps that resembled the whole world as we know it appeared in the sixteenth century, following the great expeditions of Christopher Columbus and others. Today's sophisticated aerial and satellite photography means that we can chart the planet with great precision—we can also monitor changes in the shapes of the polar ice caps caused by global warming and observe the effects of disasters.

LOCATION, LOCATION

Before the invention of the telescope, astronomers and navigators developed other devices to help their work. For centuries they used a mechanical device called the astrolabe to calculate movements on the celestial sphere. Usually fashioned in metal, the classic astrolabe bears a striking resemblance in form and function to the planisphere included at the front of your book. Other measuring tools included the quadrant and sextant, which stellar surveyors used to check angles in the heavens.

Positions on Earth's surface are given in latitude and longitude, measured from pole to pole and around the circumference, respectively. The prime meridian, or 0° line of longitude, runs

EARTH'S AXIS

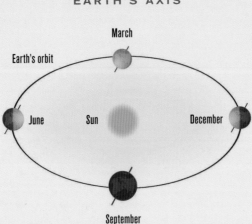

The tilt of Earth's axis gives us our seasons, with the northern and southern hemispheres each slowly turning toward and away from the Sun over the course of a year.

through London's historic Royal Observatory at Greenwich, which was founded to help sailors find their longitude at sea. Latitude was simple enough but longitude was difficult because Earth rotates, and so it was essential to have a precise measure of the time. To aid them, in the eighteenth-century clockmaker John Harrison invented a series of mechanical chronometers that would remain accurate on long voyages. Today's atomic clocks give time with ultra-precision, and satellites are used for positioning.

SHIFTING STARS

Unlike the Sun, the positions of the other stars are unaffected by our orbital journey, appearing in the same position in the sky every night 23 hours 56 minutes later. This interval is called a sidereal day. You can see the effect of this when you dial different dates and times using the planisphere included with this book.

TIME SHIFT

Simple shadow-casting sticks evolved into sundials, which were the earliest clocks. They make great timepieces because you never have to wind them up. But these devices, using the shadow of a gnomon to mark the hour, regularly run fast or slow. That is because Earth's orbit is not circular and so it travels at varying speeds, as Kepler's laws dictated. Plotted against the sky at the same time each day, the Sun would appear to describe a figure eight, called the analemma, over the course of the year, because of Earth's changing orbital speed plus the changing altitude of the Sun through the seasons.

TRIP AROUND THE SUN

The exact time Earth takes to complete one orbit of the Sun is actually 365 days 6 hours 9 minutes 9.54 seconds, which is why we have regular leap years to make up the difference that the additional hours make to the calendar.

The analemma. Regular photos of the Sun taken at the same time of day over a year reveal the figure-eight pattern—the analemma—over ancient Delphi, Greece.

A GLOBAL JIGSAW

The continents look a bit like pieces of a jigsaw, in which, for instance, Africa might fit snugly up against the Americas. This is something that must have been noticed when the earliest accurate maps of the world were produced. However, the first record of any theory to explain this did not emerge until the nineteenth century.

The blue planet. Earth appears like a blue marble, unlike any other planet, in this image built up from many photos taken by NASA spacecraft.

MOVING CONTINENTS

In 1858 American Antonio Snider suggested that a single huge land mass had broken up to cause the biblical flood. In 1912 German scientist Alfred Wegener proposed that the continents were drifting. He was met with ridicule, and for decades schools continued to teach, incorrectly, that Earth was like a shriveled orange and that mountains were like wrinkles on the surface.

Today we know that continents are riding like rafts on a global network of tectonic plates and have been doing so since Earth formed. Some 300 million years ago they all collided to form one giant land mass that scientists have called Pangaea, meaning "entire earth" in ancient Greek. A hundred million years later this supercontinent began to break up, though North America was still joined to Europe 65 million years ago, as was Australia to Antarctica and South America.

TIME AND TIDE

The Moon and, to a lesser extent, the Sun both exert a considerable pull on our planet, most evident in the regular motion of the seas that we call the tides. What is less obvious is a movement in Earth's crust caused by the same gravitational forces.

CONSTANT UPHEAVAL

At the edges of tectonic plates, we find either new hot rock rising from within Earth or old rock being driven back underground, producing ocean trenches. Mountain ranges form when a continent wrinkles up at the edge of a colliding plate, and fault lines occur where the plates rub against each other. These zones are often marked by strings of volcanoes and the regular occurrence of earthquakes, where the strains felt by colliding plates are suddenly released in waves of seismic energy.

Major fault lines run through a number of heavily populated areas, including the coast of California, Japan, and the west coast of South America. The human tragedy that quakes inflict has led scientists to try to find ways to predict their occurrence. At present, seismic detectors can give only a few minutes' notice, but new research suggests that satellites might register up to two weeks' warning by detecting electrical energy radiating from rocks under pressure. There have been reports of brilliant lights in the sky before large earthquakes.

DID THE EARTH MOVE?

The periodic shaking within Earth's crust that results in devastating earthquakes must have been as terrifying in ancient times as it is today. The ancient Chinese explained earthquakes through the opposing forces of yin and yang, and the ancient Greeks thought they might be caused by water driving through underground hollows or large areas of wet earth drying out.

ANIMAL INSTINCTS

Controversial evidence suggests that many animals become strangely agitated in the hours before an earthquake strikes. A devastating quake in China in 2008 was preceded by mass migrations of frogs and toads and anxious pacing about by captive pandas. Other imminent seismic events are said to have upset a range of animals.

The earthquake of April 18, 1906, devastated San Francisco when the northernmost 296 miles (477 km) of the San Andreas fault ruptured.

EYES IN THE SKY

Hundreds of artificial satellites now orbit Earth. Apart from those observing the sky or carrying television and other communications signals, there are dozens that constantly watch our planet. Many are top-secret military surveillance devices, but others check the weather and environment, search for mineral reserves, or aid mapping and navigation. The Global Positioning System (GPS) that allows travelers to pinpoint their exact positions uses a constellation of orbiting satellites that were originally developed for military purposes.

TECTONIC PLATES

Permian
225 million years ago

Triassic
200 million years ago

Jurassic
135 million years ago

Cretaceous
65 million years ago

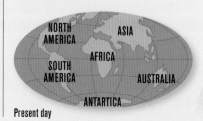

Present day

SOMETHING IN THE AIR

Earth is surrounded by the band of gases that make up the atmosphere. Billions of years ago this would have been deadly poisonous, but the earliest organisms produced vast amounts of oxygen, creating the breathable atmosphere we have today.

IT'S A GAS

Oxygen makes up 21 percent of the atmosphere, with nitrogen the most dominant gas at 78 percent. Argon and a mix of other gases form the remaining 1 percent.

The Moon shines faintly through Earth's upper atmosphere above a mass of clouds in a photo from orbit.

THROUGH THICK AND THIN

The atmosphere gradually becomes thinner as you go higher, and it becomes difficult to breathe once you reach more than 2 miles (3 km) above sea level. Tourist space flights are aiming to fly to a height of 62 miles (100 km), but traces of atmosphere can still be detected 370 miles (600 km) above Earth. Atmospheric pressure—the weight of air—falls as the atmosphere thins with increased altitude.

The lowest part of the atmosphere is the troposphere. Warming by the sun puts this layer in constant motion, causing the winds and weather. About 30 miles (48 km) up, a still region called the stratosphere begins. It includes the ozone layer, discovered in only 1913, which blocks most of the Sun's harmful ultraviolet rays. After this, and extending to a height of 50 miles (80 km), comes the mesosphere, where temperatures drop, followed by the thermosphere, where they rapidly rise again because of the Sun's energy.

A MAGNETIC PERSONALITY

Those clever ancient Greeks knew that some stones were natural magnets, and the Chinese found, in about A.D. 1000, that a suspended, magnetized needle will line up in a certain direction. This was the birth of the compass. William Gilbert, physician to Queen Elizabeth I of England, established that Earth was effectively a giant magnet.

In 1958, the satellite Explorer 1 discovered two zones of radiation circling the world. They were named the Van Allen Belts, after the American scientist James Van Allen, who led the mission. It began to be understood that the belts lay at the heart of a huge protective blanket, Earth's magnetic field, which steers away the stream of dangerous energy from the Sun called the solar wind. Astrophysicist Thomas Gold named this shield the magnetosphere in 1959. On the Sun-facing side of Earth, the magnetosphere is squashed down, but it becomes very stretched on the opposite side. An inner layer of the magnetosphere is the ionosphere, which is made up of highly charged plasma that helps to bounce radio signals over long distances.

LIGHT SHOWS

The bombardment of particles from explosions on the Sun causes a dramatic and sometimes colorful display called the aurora borealis (northern lights) or aurora australis (southern lights). These are seen most often at high latitudes around the poles, but the biggest displays reach much lower latitudes on rare occasions. French philosopher Pierre Gassendi used the term "aurora borealis" in 1621, after it was first suggested by Galileo in 1619. A Norwegian scientist, Kristian Birkeland, working in the late nineteenth and early twentieth centuries, explained why the aurora happens by aiming a stream of charged particles at a magnetic model of Earth in a vacuum chamber. They all veered toward its poles. Electrons in the real aurora were not detected until a rocket was flown into them in 1954.

CLIMATE OF FEAR

Water vapor and other gases keep Earth warm by trapping the Sun's heat like a greenhouse. Many fear that man-made forces are exaggerating this effect, and that excessive global warming is altering weather patterns and melting the ice caps, causing sea levels to rise. Others believe that man's influence is tiny compared with greater forces—solar activity, for example—that have produced major climatic changes in the past, including the ice ages.

CLOUDING THE VIEW

Until recent decades, telescopic observations of the stars and planets had to be made through the atmosphere. Astronomers were at the mercy of the clouds, but even if skies *were* clear, their views were often distorted by air currents, water vapor, haze, or pollution. Today many astronomical observatories are satellites in space, where they are free from such problems. They also escape the modern-day curse of light pollution. The growth of industry and the determination of many towns and cities to turn night into day with excessive lighting have robbed many of us of our right to a dark-sky window on the universe.

Northern lights. A dramatic display of the aurora borealis lights up the sky over Bear Lake, Alaska.

Let there be light. Mankind reveals his presence with the lights of major population centers in a NASA image of Earth by night.

CHAPTER FOUR

THE MOON

Of all the bodies in the solar system, the Moon has always held a special place for us. It is the fifth largest satellite of any planet, and its proximity to Earth means that it shines as a giant orb, and we can clearly see features on its surface. It is also the only other world that humans have visited.

The power of the Moon affects Earth, its gravitational pull being the main cause of our oceans' tides. But the Moon has also influenced areas other than science. It has inspired poets and musicians—a full moon casting her shimmering light on the water is a romantic image as powerful as the idea that our nearest neighbor can awaken werewolves or bring out "lunacy" in people.

Earth is the first planet from the Sun to have a natural satellite and, at more than a quarter the diameter of Earth, the Moon is so large that we have been considered a double planet. But, whereas Earth is an active world teeming with living creatures, our celestial partner is geologically inactive and devoid of life. The Moon is a dead, sterile place—but that does not mean it is lacking in interest.

> *"The moon, like a flower*
> *In heaven's high bower,*
> *With silent delight*
> *Sits and smiles on the night."*
>
> —WILLIAM BLAKE

WHAT WE KNEW THEN

Large dark areas on the Moon are visible to the naked eye from Earth. They form the patterns that make up the face of the Man in the Moon of folklore; some people see the shapes of a rabbit or a donkey. The dark regions are called *maria*, from the Latin for "seas"—the ancient Greeks believed that these really were oceans of water.

WHAT WE THINK WE KNOW NOW

Science swiftly established that the Moon is an arid world. The lunar seas are, in fact, vast, dry plains of solidified magma that oozed from beneath the surface when the Moon still had a molten interior. For at least the past billion years, the Moon has been solid, though some believe its core might still be partly fluid.

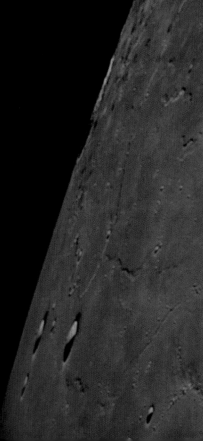

Craters and chasms stand out in stark relief in a dramatic view across the bleak landscape of our airless and sterile Moon.

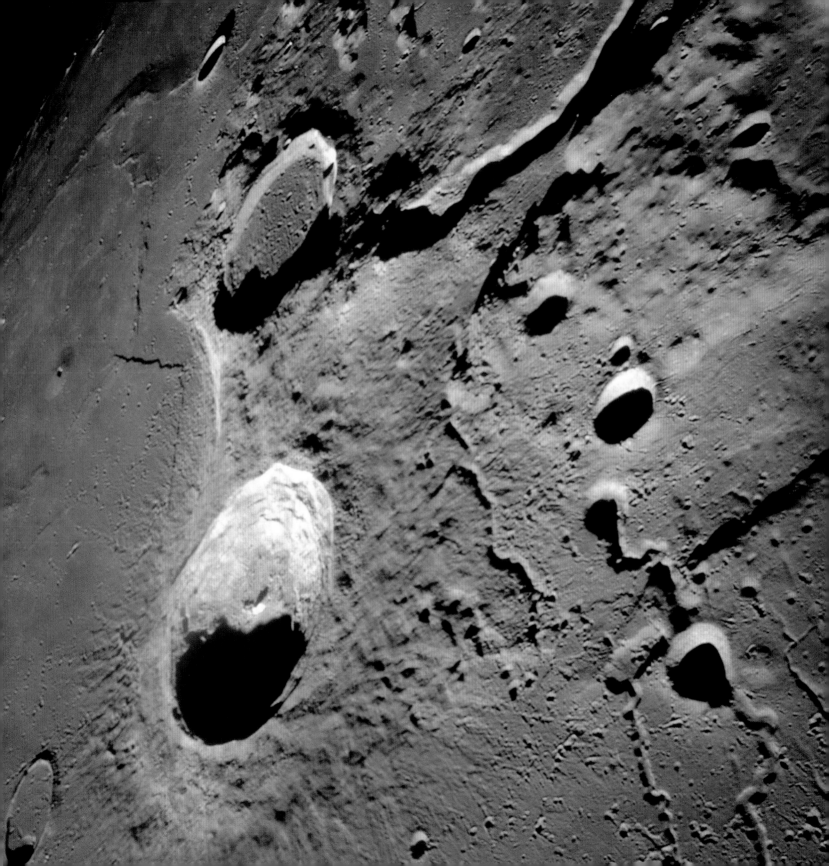

The Moon goes through several phases as its illuminated hemisphere is gradually turned toward then away from Earth.

NIGHT AND DAY

One month in our calendar is based on the time it takes the Moon to orbit Earth. In fact, it completes one elliptical orbit in slightly more than 27.3 days, waxing and waning through a range of phases. Because of Earth's own motion around the Sun, the time between one new moon and the next is more than 29.5 days.

FACE THE FACTS

The Moon has become tidally locked to Earth, which means that it always keeps the same face toward us. However, a gentle rocking of the Moon during its orbit means that we get a peek over the lunar limb at different stages of the month. This effect, called *libration*, allows us to view nearly 60 percent of the Moon's surface over time.

JUST A PHASE

The Moon shines with reflected sunlight. Half of the Moon is always in sunlight and half in darkness. At the start of the lunar month, when the Moon lies roughly between Earth and the Sun, the face we usually see is in darkness. This is new moon. As the orbit progresses, the Sun begins to rise over the near side of the Moon, producing the phases that build from crescent moon to full moon, the point at which we see it fully illuminated. The process is then reversed as the phase narrows back to new.

When the Moon is a thin crescent, the part of the Moon in darkness often becomes visible, too. Known colloquially as "the new moon in the old moon's arms," the effect is caused by sunlight reflecting off Earth and illuminating the night side of the Moon. The phenomenon, correctly explained by Leonardo da Vinci, has even been photographed during a total eclipse of the Sun.

As sunlight falls on the Moon during its orbit around Earth, it waxes and wanes to display the phases shown in the outer ring.

"I like to think that the moon is there even if I am not looking at it."
—ALBERT EINSTEIN

NOT SO BRIGHT

Though the Moon appears brilliant in the night sky—and can even be clearly seen in daylight—its surface rocks are dark. Its reflectivity, or *albedo*, is quite low, in fact. While the highlands reflect a little more than 10 percent of sunlight striking them, the figure drops to less than 5 percent for the *maria*. The full moon is much brighter than other phases because the Sun's rays are bouncing straight back at us.

THE DARK SIDE

People often speak of the "dark side of the Moon," when presumably they mean the *far* side that we never see. As a matter of fact, it's all dark—and light—in equal measure at different times. Each spot on the Moon spends nearly two weeks in light before night swiftly descends for two weeks of darkness. With no atmosphere there is no twilight, and temperatures quickly plummet from more than 212°F (100°C) in the light to below -274°F (-170°C) in the dark.

THE TERMINATOR

With a lack of lunar twilight, the line—called the terminator—between the light and dark sections of the Moon is quite distinct. Sunshine and shadows on the surface highlight the craters and mountains. Though the geographical features remain the same, the changing angle of sunlight causes their appearance from Earth to alter throughout the month. At full moon the shadows disappear, making it a poor time to view most features.

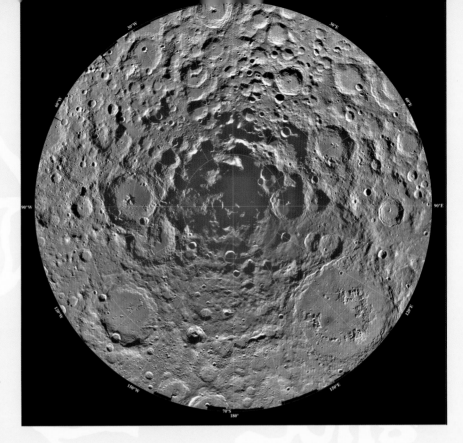

ETERNAL NIGHT

Some craters near the lunar poles have areas that never receive any sunlight. Though the Moon is arid, some believe these regions might contain water ice dumped on the Moon over billions of years by colliding comets. Space scientists plan to find out, because such reserves could provide essential supplies for future lunar colonies.

A mosaic of images from the unmanned U.S. probe *Clementine* in 1994 shows the landscape around the Moon's south pole, including craters in perpetual darkness, which might contain water ice.

The old moon in the young moon's arms shines through thin clouds soon after sunset.

A MOON IS BORN

Ancient peoples did not need to worry about how the Moon was created—to them it was simply one of the celestial gods that traversed the sky. However, as scientific knowledge advanced, people began to look for a more physical answer to explain the differences between the Moon and Earth, as well as the forces that connect them.

INSIDE THE MOON

The Moon's battered outer crust is between 30 miles (50 km) and 45 miles (75 km) deep. It is thought that beneath this it is completely solid to a depth of about 600 miles (1,000 km). Moonquakes have been recorded by detectors left on the lunar surface, and these suggest that a small metallic core may be surrounded by a partly molten region.

A 2,500-year-old bronze statuette shows how ancient Egyptians represented their moon god Iah.

A crack in the lunar crust, called a rille, photographed by astronauts aboard *Apollo 10* in May 1969 as they flew around the Moon without landing.

A world the size of Mars collides with Earth billions of years ago. Debris blasted into space by such an impact may have formed the Moon.

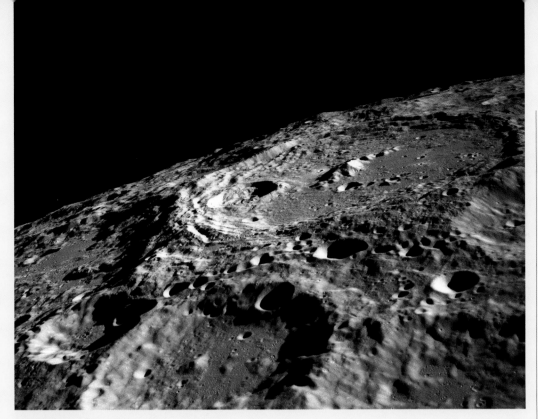

The ruggedness of the Moon's terrain is shown in this spectacular photo of craters taken from *Apollo 10* in May 1969.

CRATER SHAPES

A typical crater forms when the Moon is struck by an asteroid traveling at a very high speed. The energy released on impact vaporizes the missile in a huge explosion that blasts a hole many times bigger than the asteroid itself. Shock waves create an outer ring—the crater walls—while the rebound from the impact forms a peak at the center of the crater. The crater floor fills with a flat layer of molten rock, which then cools.

OTHER FEATURES

In addition to craters, the Moon is adorned with many other features, including mountain ranges, valleys, and steep escarpments. Trenches or cracks in the lunar crust, called rilles, can be straight or meandering like a river. Ridges that formed when the lava in the *maria* cooled look like wrinkles. Other features that are visible through telescopes include domes on the floors of craters and *maria*.

WHAT'S IN A NAME

As maps of the Moon became more detailed, cartographers used conflicting names for the features shown. In 1922 the International Astronomical Union began to impose order, and it has since controlled the nomenclature for all bodies in the solar system. Today the convention is that lunar craters are named after famous scientists, writers, philosophers, and artists.

WHAT WE KNEW THEN

A century ago it was popularly believed that the Moon was formed from a chunk of Earth. The theory ran that the young Earth was rotating so fast that it grew a huge bulge at the equator. Part of the bulge flew out into space, later solidifying as our natural satellite. This theory has now been abandoned. Also rejected are other suggestions that the Moon was a planet captured by Earth as it traveled through the solar system, or that both formed from a single conglomeration of dust.

WHAT WE THINK WE KNOW NOW

The currently accepted theory for the Moon's creation proposes that in the early violent days of the solar system, a body the size of Mars smashed into Earth. The impact blasted out a cloud of debris that formed a ring around our planet, which collected together over time to form the Moon. Astronomers like this model because it fits with their evidence. In particular, it explains why the Moon appears to have only a small iron core.

THE LUNAR LANDSCAPE

A simple glance quite clearly shows that there are dark and light regions on the Moon, but it took the invention of the telescope to reveal just how different this world is from Earth. The dark, dry "seas" (*maria*) are the lunar lowlands; the bright areas are the mountainous highlands, a granitelike crust peppered with craters.

A crude, wide-angle image from Russia's *Luna 3* spacecraft gave us our first view of the Moon's far side in October 1959.

GEOGRAPHY LESSON

The study of the Moon's geography is called selenography, Selene being the name of the moon goddess of the ancient Greeks. Some of the first sketches made from observations through a telescope were drawn by Galileo in 1609—he even tried to estimate the height of mountains from their shadows. About the same time, Thomas Harriott in England is thought to have compiled the first simple map of the Moon from his telescope observations. More detailed maps followed, with different cartographers naming features. Polish astronomer Johannes Hevelius's *Selenographia* of 1647 used terrestrial names for mountain ranges—including both Apennines and Pyrenees—that are still used today.

ANCIENT HIGHLANDS AND WATERLESS SEAS

The bright mountainous regions are the older surface of the Moon, created from different kinds of volcanic rock approximately 4 billion years ago. This age is apparent from the heavy bombardment that it suffered at a stage in the solar system's development when collisions were frequent. Until the time of the Apollo missions in the 1960s and '70s, however, there was still a fierce debate about whether these craters were dead volcanoes or impact craters. Today it is accepted that the latter is the case.

The relative smoothness of the lunar *maria* shows that these regions are younger, though they were created at a time when the Moon still had a molten interior. Major asteroid impacts cracked open the lunar surface, causing magma—made of a common, dark-colored rock called basalt—to flood out. The rims of some of the larger craters that were engulfed by this lava flow can still be seen poking out of the smooth surface.

Thousands of photos from the Clementine probe are combined to produce a detailed picture of the lunar far side, revealing it to be unlike the side that faces us.

A beautifully drawn map of the Moon, with south at the top, was produced by a German cartographer, Richard Andree, in 1881.

THE FAR SIDE

Because the Moon always presents the same face to Earth, it was not until 1959 that we discovered what the other side looked like. The first images were taken by a Soviet probe called *Luna 3*, and its historic pictures, though crude, were surprising because they revealed an almost total lack of *maria*. The reason was found to be that the lunar crust is about 15 miles (25 km) thicker on the far side, which made it more difficult for magma to reach the surface following an impact.

LUNAR TOPSOIL

Early space artists painted very jagged-looking mountains and craters on the Moon, which is how they appeared through the telescope. However, the first manned missions found the surface to be more rounded than expected. This is because a steady bombardment of the surface by tiny meteoroid particles over billions of years has steadily worn the surface down, pulverizing the rock to create a surface layer of rubble a few yards deep that is a kind of lunar topsoil.

Before the Apollo landings, there were fears that dust on the surface of the Moon would be so deep that astronauts and landing probes might sink into it. Those fears proved unfounded, but space scientists are now concerned that the potentially toxic moon dust, which Apollo astronauts said smelled of gunpowder, clings readily to everything and might get into people's lungs. Lunar dust and soil is, however, expected to have a useful role in helping build bricks for lunar colonies' construction sites.

IMPACTS TODAY

Surprisingly, it was not until 2005 that astronomers realized they could still see lunar impacts taking place. The kinds of meteoroids that burn up as shooting stars when they hit Earth's atmosphere reach the Moon's surface unscathed. The resulting impact causes a mini-explosion, and if the missile is big enough and hits the night side of the Moon, this blast is visible from Earth. A NASA team now monitors these impacts and is recording dozens every year.

With no lunar atmosphere to burn them up, meteoroid impacts pose a small but real hazard for future astronauts.

One of the earliest attempts to map the Moon was made by Johannes Hevelius in 1647. North is at the top.

A CANTERBURY TALE

A medieval English monk named Gervase of Canterbury reported that in 1178 an impact on the Moon "spewed out fire, hot coals and sparks." Some scientists have suggested this event was the creation of the youngest crater known on the Moon, Giordano Bruno. At the start of the twenty-first century, American scientists decided, however, that Gervase must have seen a normal fireball that just happened to be in line with the Moon, since a lunar impact would have caused a week-long blizzard of shooting stars over Earth.

PHOTOS AND FOOTPRINTS

The first detailed photograph through a telescope was taken in 1839 by John William Draper, an English-born chemistry professor in New York. His daguerreotype clearly shows the main features visible on a full moon, including the prominent impact crater Tycho.

This image of *Apollo 11* astronaut Buzz Aldrin's footprint was taken to help study the nature of lunar dust.

SNAPPING OUR SATELLITE

After Draper, astronomers seized upon the new medium of photography, and by the end of the nineteenth century the quality of images had improved considerably. A number of photographic atlases of the Moon were compiled using powerful telescopes during the early decades of the twentieth century.

First men on the Moon. Neil Armstrong captures his own shadow and fellow astronaut Buzz Aldrin by the lunar module in July 1969.

After the Soviet *Luna 3* pictures, the United States followed with three *Ranger* probes in the early 1960s that took photographs of the near side before crashing. As that decade progressed, U.S. *Surveyor* probes landed and produced pictures from the surface, while mapping from above the Moon was made by five Lunar Orbiter craft.

FLIGHTS OF FANCY

There are ancient legends, including Chinese folklore, describing journeys to the Moon. But the first person to write seriously about the idea was Johannes Kepler, the pioneering planetary scientist who, in 1630, imagined a launch using "demon power." Not long after, the French writer Cyrano de Bergerac wrote a story about flying to the Moon propelled by the rising dew. Lunar voyages became an increasingly popular science-fiction theme, as shown in the works of those classic writers of the genre Jules Verne (*From the Earth to the Moon*, 1865) and H. G. Wells (*The First Men in the Moon*, 1901).

DIGITAL DELIGHTS

Detailed mapping of the Moon had to wait until NASA's 1994 probe *Clementine*, which took 1.8 million digital photographs, including images of the previously neglected poles. A follow-up, *Prospector*, scanned the Moon at other wavelengths to help identify minerals on the surface. ESA's *SMART-1* probe in 2003 looked for evidence of ice in the polar shadows before being crashed deliberately so that ground telescopes could try to identify any buried water.

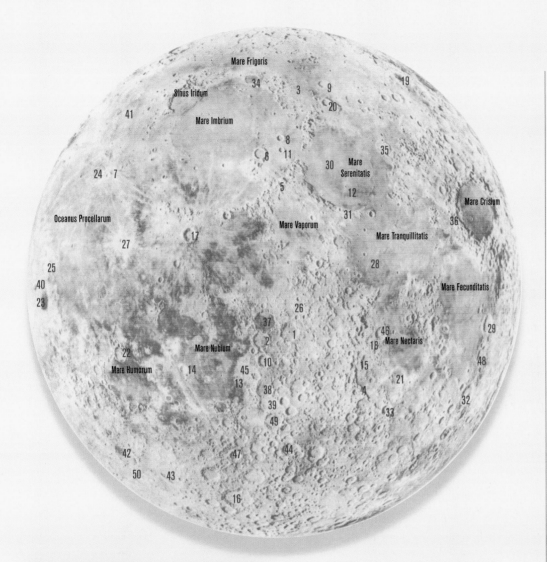

Mare Frigoris

34

Sinus Iridum

41

Mare Imbrium

24 7

Oceanus Procellarum

27

17

25

40

23

22

Mare Humorum

14

Mare Nubium

42

50 43

16

3   9

20

8

6   11

5

30   Mare
      Serenitatis

35

12

31   Mare Vaporum

37
2
1

10

45

13

38

39

49

47   44

26

18   Mare Nectaris

15

4

21   33

19

Mare Crisium

36

Mare Tranquillitatis

28

Mare Fecunditatis

46

29

48

32

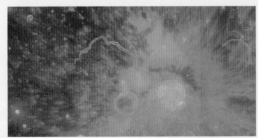

Color filters allowed instruments on the *Clementine* probe to study the mineral makeup of the Moon, including this region around the crater Aristarchus.

BACK TO THE MOON

More than three decades after humans last walked on the surface of the Moon, the United States is looking to send manned missions there by 2020. NASA is designing an Orion command module, which will be three times the size of the one used for the Apollo missions, and a new lunar module that will help astronauts prepare the ground for future lunar colonies.

ECLIPSES OF THE SUN

By remarkable chance, the Moon and the Sun appear the same size in the sky from Earth. Appearances are deceptive, of course, as the Sun is really 400 times the diameter of the Moon, and the effect is due to the latter being so much closer to us. This coincidence offers us the occasional incredible spectacle of a total eclipse of the Sun.

Prominences and the brighter regions of the Sun's ghostly corona come into view in this photo of a total eclipse taken in March 2006 over Turkey.

DEVOURING THE SUN

Ancient peoples found eclipses of the Sun to be terrifying occurrences. It appeared as if a sky monster—a dragon in India, Indonesia, and China, a vampire in Siberia, or a giant frog in Vietnam—was devouring the giver of light and heat. Arrows were fired and drums banged to ward off the evil beast, an approach that, invariably, was found to work. Today, with the cause fully understood, eclipses can be precisely predicted. However, they still evoke awe and wonder, and astronomers travel the world to catch them at their best.

Reports of solar eclipses can be found in Chinese records that are more than 4,000 years old, when court astrologers His and Ho were beheaded for failing to predict one in 2134 B.C. A similar event halted a battle between the Lydians and the Medes in 585 B.C. Other eclipses are mentioned in the Bible (736 B.C.) and Homer's *Odyssey*, which may refer to an eclipse that occurred over Greece in 1178 B.C. Linking ancient eclipse dates with the places where they were observed allows scientists to measure the change over time in Earth's rotation. This can also help historians date other nonastronomical events by working out when the eclipse took place.

The Moon's apparent size varies at different stages in its elliptical orbit. When farthest from Earth, it is too small to cover the Sun completely. This is known as an annular eclipse because the Sun appears as a bright ring (annulus), around the edge of the Moon.

HOW ECLIPSES HAPPEN

As science replaced superstition, it was realized that solar eclipses were caused by the new moon passing between Earth and the Sun. When the Moon completely covers the Sun, it casts a main shadow, the umbra, that may be roughly 100 miles (160 km) wide on Earth. As the Moon orbits and Earth rotates, this shadow can trace a track thousands of miles long on the ground. On either side of this narrow track, in the penumbral shadow, the Moon only partly covers the Sun. This is termed a partial eclipse and is visible over a far greater area.

Special solar glasses allow an onlooker to view a partial eclipse of the Sun safely from London in August 2008.

As the Moon begins to pass in front of the Sun, it appears to take an ever bigger bite out of it. When a large part of the Sun is covered, the temperature will drop markedly and daylight will take on a peculiar hue. In the last moments before totality—as the moment of full eclipse is called—some final glimpses of the Sun may be seen momentarily shining through valleys on the edge of the Moon, a phenomenon called Baily's Beads in honor of the British astronomer Francis Baily, who first noted the phenomenon in 1836. Darkness falls suddenly as the Moon's shadow rushes across the ground.

TOTAL MAGIC

Totality can last from a few seconds to a little more than 7 minutes. Stars and planets may be seen in the dark sky, and bright red flamelike prominences peek out from behind the edge of the Moon. This is also a rare opportunity to see the glow of the solar atmosphere, the corona, normally invisible because of the Sun's overpowering brightness. Bright streamers may be seen within this ghostly glow. Totality is ended suddenly by the diamond-ring effect, caused when the brilliant flash of sunlight reappears.

CHASING ECLIPSES

Astronomers used to embark on long voyages to witness total eclipses of the Sun. Today, however, special cruises make unusual vacations for amateur eclipse watchers, while professionals charter jets to chase the Moon's shadow around the globe and so extend the amount of totality that they can study.

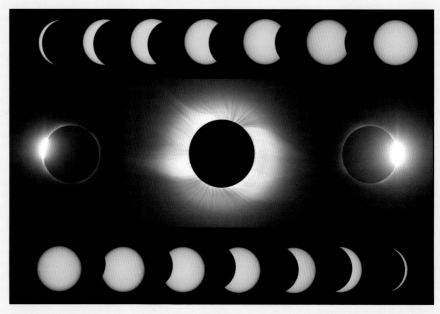

A dramatic sequence of images shows how the total eclipse of the Sun appeared over Siberia on August 1, 2008.

TOTAL ECLIPSE OF THE SUN

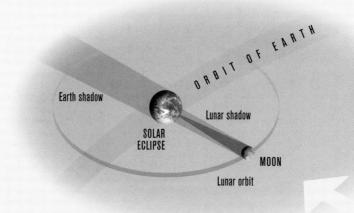

Earth shadow

ORBIT OF EARTH

Lunar shadow

SOLAR ECLIPSE

MOON

Lunar orbit

Direction of sunlight

The celestial lineup that produces a total eclipse of the Sun. A partial eclipse is visible from within the lighter shadow zone.

ECLIPSES OF THE MOON

Eclipses of the Moon were equally alarming to our ancestors. The familiar bright silvery light of a full moon would suddenly and inexplicably begin to take on a blood red hue. Today we know that the Moon is simply passing through Earth's shadow. Lunar eclipses are viewed as interesting spectacles rather than events from which astronomers can learn.

During a total lunar eclipse the Moon turns a shade of red because Earth's atmosphere blocks any blue light.

When a full moon lines up directly with Earth and the Sun, it enters our planet's shadow producing a lunar eclipse.

INTO THE SHADOWS

Earth casts a cone-shaped shadow in space—the same shadow that gives us night. Like the one caused on Earth by eclipses of the Sun, this shadow has a dark center called the umbra, which is circled by a lighter ring called the penumbra. If you could stand on the Moon inside the penumbra, the Sun would appear to be only partly covered by Earth. During any lunar eclipse the Moon must first move into the penumbra—in about one third of eclipses, the Moon only passes through this lighter band and so does not dim significantly.

ECLIPSE IN PROGRESS

If the Moon moves into the umbra either partly (a partial eclipse) or fully (a total eclipse), the effect is obvious. The Moon will turn a deep orange or red and can sometimes even disappear from view altogether. The color and brightness depend on the amount of volcanic ash in our atmosphere, because the Moon during an eclipse is only visible because of sunlight scattered onto it through our own atmosphere. In the mid-twentieth century, astronomer André-Louis Danjon devised a five-point scale for describing the brightness of a total lunar eclipse.

TOTAL ECLIPSE OF THE MOON

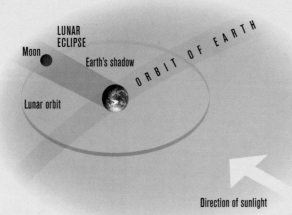

LUNAR ECLIPSE

Moon

Earth's shadow

ORBIT OF EARTH

Lunar orbit

Direction of sunlight

DANJON'S FIVE-POINT SCALE

L = 0   Very dark eclipse; Moon almost invisible, especially at mid-totality

L = 1   Dark eclipse, gray or brownish in coloration; details distinguishable only with difficulty

L = 2   Deep red or rust-colored eclipse; very dark central shadow, while outer edge of umbra relatively bright

L = 3   Brick red eclipse; umbral shadow usually has a bright or yellow rim

L = 4   Very bright copper-red or orange eclipse; umbral shadow has a bluish, very bright rim

SOLAR ECLIPSES (2009–2020)

Date	Type	Where
2009 January 26	Annular	southern Africa, Antarctica, southeastern Asia, Australia
2009 July 22	Total	eastern Asia, Pacific, Hawaii
2010 January 15	Annular	Africa, Asia
2010 July 11	Total	southern South America
2012 May 20	Annular	Asia, Pacific, North America
2012 November 13	Total	Australia, New Zealand, southern Pacific, southern South America
2013 May 10	Annular	Australia, New Zealand, central Pacific
2014 April 29	Annular	southern India, Australia, Antarctica
2015 March 20	Total	Iceland, Europe, northern Africa, northern Asia
2016 March 9	Total	eastern Asia, Australia, Pacific
2016 September 1	Annular	Africa, Indian Ocean
2017 February 26	Annular	southern South America, Atlantic, Africa, Antarctica
2017 August 21	Total	North America, northern South America
2019 July 2	Total	southern Pacific, South America
2019 December 26	Annular	Asia, Australia
2020 June 21	Annular	Africa, southeastern Europe, Asia
2020 December 14	Total	Pacific, southern South America, Antarctica

LUNAR ECLIPSES (2009–2020)

Date	Type	Where
2009 December 31	Partial	Europe, Africa, Asia, Australia
2010 June 26	Partial	eastern Asia, Australia, Pacific, western Americas
2010 December 21	Total	eastern Asia, Australia, Pacific, Americas, Europe
2011 June 15	Total	South America, Europe, Africa, Asia, Australia
2011 December 10	Total	Europe, eastern Africa, Asia, Australia, Pacific
2012 June 4	Partial	Asia, Australia, Pacific, Americas
2013 April 25	Partial	Europe, Africa, Asia, Australia
2014 April 15	Total	Australia, Pacific, Americas
2014 October 8	Total	Asia, Australia, Pacific, Americas
2015 April 4	Total	Asia, Australia, Pacific, Americas
2015 September 28	Total	eastern Pacific, Americas, Europe, Africa, western Asia
2017 August 7	Partial	Europe, Africa, Asia, Australia
2018 January 31	Total	Asia, Australia, Pacific, western North America
2018 July 27	Total	South America, Europe, Africa, Asia, Australia
2019 January 21	Total	central Pacific, Americas, Europe, Africa
2019 July 16	Partial	South America, Europe, Africa, Asia, Australia

The Moon slowly slips into the shadow of Earth during a lunar eclipse in January 2000.

CHAPTER FIVE

MERCURY

Mercury, the closest globe to the Sun, is the smallest of the rocky, terrestrial planets. It is smaller, even, than the largest moons orbiting Jupiter and Saturn—Ganymede and Titan. Named after the winged messenger of the Roman gods, Mercury is one of the five planets known to the ancients, though its proximity to the Sun and its rapid motion meant they obtained only occasional glimpses of it in their twilight skies. It has never been hard to imagine the searing heat that the areas of Mercury exposed to the Sun must endure.

However, our knowledge of what that world is really like had to wait until 1974 when the first probe to that part of the solar system, *Mariner 10*, paid a visit and photographed mountains, craters, and peculiar ridges. Another mission, *Messenger*, began to put Mercury under scrutiny once again in 2008, and two more probes are set to circle the planet in the next decade. This is greatly enhancing our understanding of Mercury as we map its surface, discover the nature of its interior, and even gain clues to the planet's possibly violent birth.

"This flyby allowed us to see a part of the planet never before viewed by spacecraft, and our little craft has returned a gold mine of exciting data."

—Sean Solomon, Principal Investigator for the Messenger Mission

WHAT WE KNEW THEN

Mercury has long been compared with our Moon. Both are rocky, cratered worlds, and Mercury also shows phases when viewed in a telescope. At one time astronomers thought Mercury had a day the same length as its year so that it always kept the same scorched face toward the Sun, just as the Moon does to Earth.

WHAT WE THINK WE KNOW NOW

Mercury may superficially resemble the Moon, but there are clear differences. The planet's day is shorter than its year, so that all sides face the Sun—rather like a chicken on a spit. Unlike the Moon, however, Mercury has a tenuous atmosphere and a molten interior, so that it is, perhaps, fundamentally more like Earth.

With merely a hint of an atmosphere, sunrise on Mercury is wildly different to any on Earth, as searing heat roasts the rocky terrain.

ELUSIVE MERCURY

Mercury is rarely easy to find, even though it is one of the brightest objects in the sky. The problem is that its proximity to the Sun means it never wanders far from our parent star when viewed from Earth.

Mercury shines through a gap in the clouds low after sunset over Sandwich in southeast England.

SAFETY FIRST

To see Mercury, you must catch it soon after sunset or shortly before sunrise when it appears farthest from the Sun at one of its greatest elongations—but it will still be hugging the horizon. If you are blessed with the right conditions—a clear sky and an obstruction-free horizon—Mercury can shine clearly, and you will wonder how you ever missed it. But most people go through life without ever seeing this elusive planet. Being so close to the Sun can present a serious hazard in trying to observe Mercury. If you try to sweep the sky with binoculars to find it, protect your eyes by looking only when the Sun is below the horizon.

GOING THE DISTANCE

Mercury's orbit is more elliptical than any of the seven other planets—its distance from the Sun ranges from 28.58 million miles (46.01 million km) to 43.38 million miles (69.84 million km). The main axis of this orbit, joining the closest and farthest points, slowly rotates around the Sun over time. Some saw this as evidence that another undiscovered planet lay between Mercury and the Sun, which was pulling on the little globe. However, we now know that the effect—called the advance of perihelion—is a naturally occurring phenomenon.

This hypothetical undiscovered planet was named Vulcan. An avid believer was the nineteenth-century mathematician Urbain le Verrier, fresh from his success in predicting the existence of Neptune from its pull on Uranus. Many observers claimed to have seen Vulcan crossing the Sun or during a solar eclipse, but these proved to be false alarms, mistaking sunspots or stars for the non-existent planet.

SUBTLE SHADINGS

Amateur astronomers have long tried to detect features on the surface of Mercury, but they have only ever been able to sketch different levels of shading, indicating lighter or darker regions, even when observed through large telescopes. Mercury never appears larger than 13 seconds of arc in diameter, and Galileo's telescopes were unable to reveal its moonlike phases. No ground-based telescope can ever hope to show details such as the craters, ridges, and mountains that we now know cover the planet.

Subtle shadings on Mercury are recorded in sketches by an experienced amateur astronomer viewing the planet through a 6-inch (15-cm) refracting telescope.

ELONGATIONS

Eastern elongations occur in the evening and western elongations in the morning. The greatest distance Mercury can reach at one of these is 28 degrees. The best time to look is when the ecliptic is steeply inclined to the horizon, on spring evenings and fall mornings from middle latitudes.

The following list shows elongations where Mercury will travel more than 25 degrees from the Sun:

2009 February 13 (morning)
2009 August 24 (evening)
2010 May 26 (morning)
2010 August 7 (evening)
2011 May 7 (morning)
2011 July 20 (evening)
2012 April 18 (morning)
2012 July 1 (evening)
2013 March 31 (morning)
2013 October 9 (evening)
2014 March 14 (morning)
2014 September 21 (evening)
2015 February 24 (morning)
2015 September 4 (evening)

MERCURY'S ORBIT

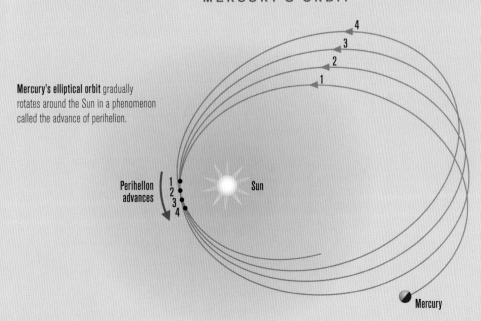

Mercury's elliptical orbit gradually rotates around the Sun in a phenomenon called the advance of perihelion.

Perihelion advances

Sun

Mercury

A DENSE WORLD

Mercury has a very large and partly liquid iron core, which is thought to be three-quarters of the total diameter of the planet. Recent studies suggest that Mercury may have been struck by another planet-sized body billions of years ago, which stripped away much of its outer mantle. The impact would have been so colossal that Earth would have been spattered with the debris. Another theory claims that the Sun vaporized the outer layers of Mercury as it condensed in size during the early days of the solar system.

A MAGNETIC MESSAGE

When the *Messenger* probe flew through Mercury's magnetic field in January 2008, it detected charged particles of silicon, sodium, sulfur, and even water ions, blasted from the planet's surface and atmosphere by the solar wind. This treasure trove suggests that volcanic processes played a major part in creating that material.

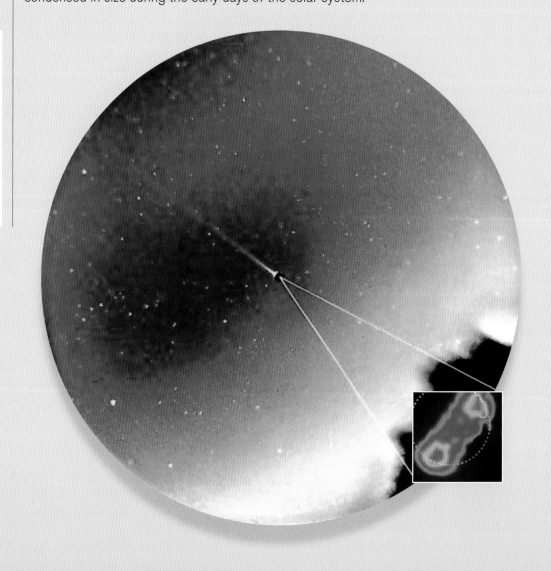

An Earthbound telescope fitted with sophisticated imaging equipment reveals Mercury's tail of sodium gas being stripped away by the solar wind. Inset, in false colors, are the source regions of the gases that the *Messenger* probe also detected in 2008.

PULLING POWER

The density of Mercury was first determined in 1841 by the German astronomer Johann Franz Encke, who produced a figure that is within 20 percent of today's best measurements. The technique he employed was to check the effect of the planet's gravitational pull on a comet that makes frequent flights through the inner solar system. The celestial visitor now carries his name as Comet Encke. In 2007 U.S. astronomers used three radio telescopes to bounce radar signals off Mercury and confirm that it has a liquid core. Their technique was similar to the way you can test whether an egg is soft inside or hard boiled simply by spinning it—a hard-boiled egg will spin more freely.

DAYLIGHT ROBBERY

As late as the 1960s, astronomers thought Mercury had a trapped rotation—meaning that it presented the same side to the Sun during orbit—just as the Moon always shows the same face to Earth. If this was correct, it would have meant that Mercury had a day that was 88 Earth days long and a permanent dark side. But in 1965, by bouncing radar waves off the planet, astronomers discovered that Mercury actually spins once in about 59 Earth days, meaning it has three days every two local years. Thanks to its highly elliptical orbit, the Sun must seem to make a slow and erratic journey across the sky when observed from the surface of Mercury, even appearing to reverse direction briefly at times.

AIR AND ACTIVITY

Mercury has an extremely thin atmosphere, composed mainly of helium and hydrogen from the solar wind. It also has a weak magnetic blanket, confirming its molten-iron interior and indicating that active geological processes are still going on underground. In this respect Mercury is again very different from the Moon.

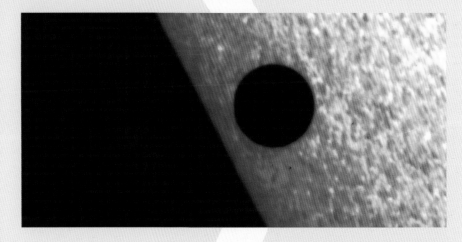

TRANSITS OF MERCURY

Occasionally it is possible to view Mercury away from Earth's horizon—during the total phase of an eclipse of the Sun, for example, or during transits, when Mercury can be seen crossing the face of the Sun. Because Mercury's orbit is not exactly level with our own, these occur more rarely than might be expected, and only in May or November. May events happen at intervals of 13 and 33 years and November transits at intervals of 7, 13, and 33 years. The last occurred on November 8, 2006, and there will not be another until May 9, 2016.

The sun-watching space telescope Hinode captures the silhouette of Mercury passing in front of the Sun's disk on November 8, 2006.

A RUGGED LANDSCAPE

> *"Mercury was not the planet we expected. It's a very dynamic place with a lot going on."*
>
> —SEAN SOLOMON, PRINCIPAL INVESTIGATOR FOR THE MESSENGER MISSION

Until the development of the telescope, Mercury could only ever be seen as a bright "star." But the power of the magnifying lens revealed that this world displayed phases like the Moon. It was impossible to make out any detail, though sharp-eyed observers sketched some subtle tonal variations on the tiny dot. Mercury's phases were clear evidence that it must lie between Earth and the Sun.

A NONLUNAR LANDSCAPE

Images sent home from *Mariner 10*'s three flybys of Mercury in 1974 revealed a rugged, heavily cratered landscape that, at first, seemed like the Moon. However, *Mariner* revealed that Mercury is also crossed by numerous ridges, with cliffs 1 mile (1.6 km) or more high that resemble nothing on the Moon and snake for hundreds of miles across the terrain. Some believe these wrinkles may be faults caused when Mercury cooled and shrank, like a dried, shriveled orange; others think they are formed by sheets of rising volcanic magma.

A GREATER CRATER

One major surprise from the *Mariner 10* flybys was the discovery that little Mercury is scarred by one of the biggest impact craters in the solar system. The Caloris Basin was at the time estimated to be about 800 miles (1,300 km) wide, but when NASA's most recent Mercury mission, Messenger, made its first flyby in January 2008, its high-resolution photographs forced scientists to revise the diameter of Caloris to an even greater 960 miles (1,545 km). It was probably created when an asteroid slammed into Mercury

Part of a scarp, or cliff, hundreds of miles long runs vertically down the right of this pockmarked region imaged by *Messenger* in 2008.

about 4 billion years ago. *Messenger* also spotted a spiderlike formation of more than 100 troughs radiating from a smaller crater in the heart of the basin.

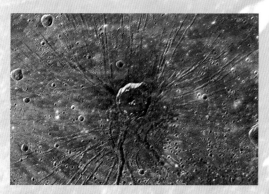

The Spider is the nickname given to this intriguing pattern of troughs that *Messenger* photographed stretching from a crater within Mercury's Caloris Basin.

A WORLD OF EXTREMES

As Mercury slowly rotates, its surface is subject to a huge range of temperatures. The side facing the Sun reaches a blistering 806°F (430°C), but when it turns into night, temperatures plunge to -292°F (-180°C). Areas within some craters near Mercury's poles appear never to experience sunlight but are highly reflective to radar beamed from Earth. Scientists speculate that despite the planet's proximity to our parent star, those regions could contain quantities of ice left long ago by impacting comets. Some of the finest photographic images from Earth have been taken by astronomers from Boston University using the Mount Wilson telescope in California. Digital enhancement revealed features not photographed by *Mariner 10* because they were on the side of the planet turned away from its camera.

An artist's view of *Mercury Planetary Orbiter*, part of the *BepiColombo* mission, which will map the inner world's surface after it arrives in late 2019.

INVASION FLEET

Mercury is about to be put under greater scrutiny than ever before. After a 4.9-billion-mile (7.9-billion-km) journey looping through the solar system, NASA's *Messenger* probe will finally enter permanent orbit around the planet in 2011. That milestone will be followed by the arrival of a joint European–Japanese mission called *BepiColombo*, which will put two probes into orbit. These craft are not due for launch until 2013, reaching Mercury six years later. Europe's orbiter will look for ice in the polar craters. Plans to add a lander to the mission were shelved to save money.

This photograph, taken from California's Mount Wilson Observatory in 1998, is the most detailed that earthbound astronomers have been able to capture.

CHAPTER SIX

VENUS

Venus, the second planet from the Sun, has long been considered Earth's sister world. It is similar in size to Earth and is rocky like our own world; no other planet comes closer. However, although it lies on our cosmic doorstep, we are only now beginning to learn the full truth about Venus, and the reality is that this is an inhospitable planet of extremes. For some reason that is yet to be fully understood, Venus veered onto a very different path from our own as it evolved.

Despite its high visibility as the brightest of the planets, Venus has hidden her secrets beneath a permanent veil of cloud. Scientists finally succeeded in penetrating this veil, first using radar and then directly with space probes. These investigations confirmed Venus to be a rocky world, but it was quite apparent that there the family likeness ends. Our sibling planet is a twisted sister where conditions are as hostile as can possibly be imagined. Venus, named after the Roman goddess of love, is in reality the neighbor from hell.

WHAT WE KNEW THEN

Early telescopes showed Galileo that Venus displayed phases like the Moon, so it was presumed that it must lie between Earth and the Sun. But, frustratingly, the permanent cloud cover meant he could only speculate what the surface looked like.

WHAT WE THINK WE KNOW NOW

At last, through the use of cloud-piercing radar, we have detailed maps of Venus, plus data about the scorched and crushing conditions on the surface, thanks to a string of space missions. We know that Venus is a planet out of control; we just need to find out why!

"In planetary terms
Venus is our nearest neighbor
but also our worst nightmare."

—ANDREW COATES,
MULLARD SPACE SCIENCE LABORATORY

Lightning crackles in the dense and poisonous atmosphere of Venus, illuminating the gloom of its permanently cloud-shrouded surface.

OBSCURED BY CLOUDS

Venus's dazzling appearance is caused by sunlight reflecting off its cloud tops. Telescope observations of its crescent phase showed that the cusps could extend farther than expected, an early indication that Venus had an atmosphere. Photos taken close to inferior conjunction showed the planet fringed by light—the glow of sunlight refracted through this atmosphere.

Sunlight illuminates the atmosphere of Venus as the planet begins its transit in front of the sun on June 8, 2004.

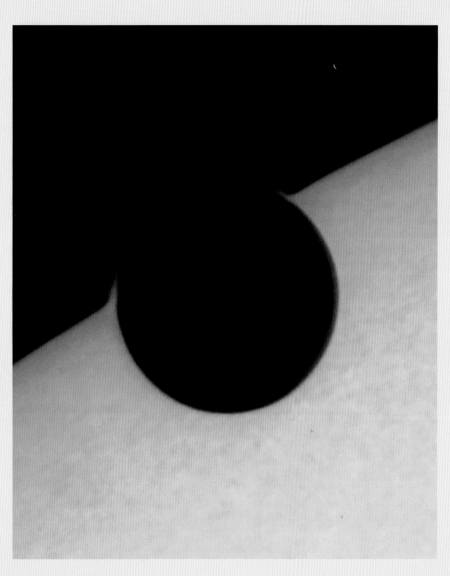

HOT PROPERTY

Venus was the first planet to be visited by space probes because scientists were eager to resolve the mystery of what lay beneath the clouds—and it was not long before they learned that Venus was no paradise. When NASA's *Mariner 2* flew past in 1962, it registered cool cloud tops but searing temperatures toward the still-invisible surface. Early attempts to reach this surface proved far more difficult than anticipated, with successive Soviet *Venera* probes losing power or being crushed. It was discovered that this was because the atmosphere was much denser than expected, with a consistency closer to water than gas. It is so heavy that air pressure at the surface is 93 times that at sea level on Earth. Life probably does not exist on Venus; but if it does, some astronomers believe that it could be drifting around in the upper clouds.

"It is really surprising how un-Earthlike Venus is now."

—PROFESSOR FRED TAYLOR,
VENUS EXPRESS SCIENTIST,
UNIVERSITY OF OXFORD

A POISONOUS PLANET

The atmosphere of Venus was discovered to be composed largely of carbon dioxide, and heavy with clouds of sulfuric acid that produce flashes of lightning. Rapid wind speeds of up to 225 miles per hour (360 kmph) were demonstrated in the V-shaped cloud patterns that revealed themselves when Venus was pictured in ultraviolet light. These wind currents include peculiar vortices over each pole. Closer to the surface, the winds drop to a slight breeze. The outer layers of Venus's atmosphere are being steadily stripped away as the planet is battered by the solar wind. And, because of its slow rotation—a Venusian day is longer than its year—this planet lacks an adequate magnetic field to protect itself from the effects of this radiation.

CLIMATE CHANGE

Though Venus's cloud tops reflect 60 percent of the Sun's heat and light, the dense atmosphere also traps the heat radiating from the planet's surface. This has produced a runaway greenhouse effect that is the most powerful known in the solar system. Scientists are intent on understanding the causes of this extreme behavior and why Venus took such a different evolutionary path from Earth. They want to learn whether the occurrences on our twin planet might have lessons for us, as we face the consequences of climate change.

VENUS EXPRESS

Europe followed the lead set by U.S. and Soviet scientists with a mission that, since 2006, has greatly added to our knowledge of Venus. Rather than mapping the surface, the *Venus Express* orbiter has concentrated on analyzing the atmosphere, studying the dynamics of the clouds and wind currents, and monitoring how the atmosphere is affected by the Sun's radiation. The mission was something of a bargain, because it reused technology designed for other space probes, in particular *Mars Express*.

Wind patterns in Venus' clouds are revealed in this ultraviolet image taken by the *Pioneer Venus Orbiter* in 1979.

Europe's *Venus Express* fires a thruster to put it into orbit around the planet in this artist's impression.

THE HIDDEN SURFACE

Before the use of cloud-piercing radar, astronomers had speculated over a range of possible landscapes for Venus. Some imagined a world covered by a constantly raging sea, while others considered the surface to be either a planet-wide sandy desert or even a lush jungle. All three scenarios were wildly wrong.

A planet-wide ocean billowing vapor was imagined by science-fiction illustrators as one possible cause for the clouds that obscured the planet.

Another completely different view of Venus was that the surface might be entirely covered by a dry and sandy desert.

LIFTING THE VEIL

We finally got our first glimpse of what the surface of Venus is really like in the 1970s, thanks to the 984-foot (300-m) radio telescope at Arecibo Observatory in Puerto Rico. Astronomers bounced radar signals off the planet to reveal two "continents"—Ishta Terra in the northern hemisphere and Aphrodite Terra in the south—plus a 36,100-foot (11,000-m) mountain that they named Maxwell Montes. More detailed radar maps of virtually the entire planet followed in the early 1990s, when NASA's *Magellan* spacecraft spent four years in orbit around Venus.

IT'S A WOMAN'S WORLD

Maxwell Montes—which was named after the nineteenth-century Scottish scientist James Clerk Maxwell—is the only feature on Venus to bear a man's name. With the exception of two regions, known as Alpha Regio and Beta Regio respectively, all other features have been named after women, taken from history or mythology. Venus itself is unique for being the only major planet to be given a feminine identity—although our home world is often referred to as Mother Earth.

LIFE IN A PRESSURE COOKER

After losing several spacecraft to Venus's hostile environment, Soviet scientists next sent two specially strengthened probes in 1975 with smaller parachutes to allow a faster descent. The *Venera 9* and *Venera 10* landers survived on the surface for 53 minutes and 65 minutes respectively, and were each able to radio home an image of their rocky surroundings before they succumbed to the punishing conditions. In 1982, *Venera 13* transmitted signals from the ground for 127 minutes, including the first color pictures.

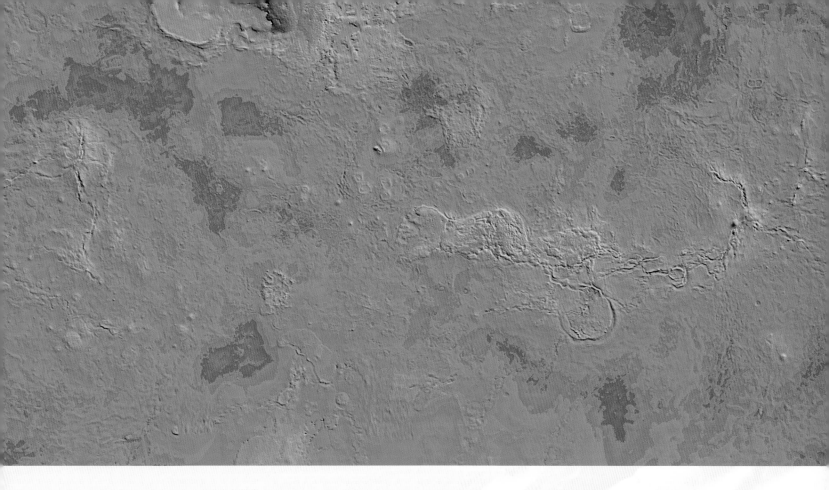

A NIGHTMARE LANDSCAPE

The surface of Venus resembles a furnace, with temperatures exceeding 870°F (470°C)—twice that found inside a domestic oven turned up to its highest setting, and hot enough to melt lead. Its vast plains are covered with many thousands of active volcanoes, which are powerful enough to resurface its planetary landscape completely over a relatively short timescale of a few hundred million years.

Despite the absence of water on Venus today, scientists believe that there may once have been oceans on the planet, just as there are on Earth. Any that did exist, however, have long since boiled away into the atmosphere and been lost into space.

Magellan's radar allowed us to produce a map of the surface of Venus, seen above in a Mercator projection with false colors to indicate different altitudes. The continents (yellow) are Ishtar Terra, at top left with its peak Maxwell Montes (red), and Aphrodite Terra just right of center. The regions around the north and south poles are shown below.

JEWEL OF THE SKIES

Venus shines like a dazzling diamond, the brightest object in the heavens other than the Sun and the Moon, but you will never see it in a midnight sky. That is because, like Mercury, the planet lies between Earth and the Sun.

TWO BECOME ONE

Venus follows the Sun down in the evening or heralds the dawn by appearing as a "morning star." Some ancient civilizations believed there these two manifestations represented separate bodies before scholars—among them Pythagoras—recognized that it is in fact one and the same. As one of the two inferior planets, Venus can be seen to go through phases just like the Moon and Mercury. It shines at its brightest when in a broad-crescent phase, not far from its closest position to Earth. It is then brilliant enough to cast shadows, though these are so subtle as to be visible only in conditions of total darkness.

DAYTIME DELIGHT

Venus becomes so bright that it may be observed in broad daylight if you know precisely where to look. Choose a day with a clear blue sky when Venus is close to one of its elongations and far from the Sun's glare. If you know the Moon to be close by, its position can help you locate the planet. It may seem a little like looking for a needle in a haystack, but once you have located Venus, you will wonder how you ever missed it.

VENUSIAN ELONGATIONS

Venus is most easily spotted from Earth when it is close to one of its greatest elongations—the points at which it appears to be farthest from the Sun. This can be as much as 47 degrees, allowing Venus to shine in a dark sky and to set up to five hours after or rise five hours before the Sun. Venus reaches its greatest elongations east when in the evening sky and its greatest elongations west in the morning sky. Here is a list of forthcoming greatest elongations:

2009 January 14 (evening)
2009 June 5 (morning)
2010 August 20 (evening)
2011 January 8 (morning)
2012 March 27 (evening)
2012 August 15 (morning)
2013 November 1 (evening)
2014 March 22 (morning)
2015 June 6 (evening)
2015 October 26 (morning)

Venus shines brilliantly over the River Thames in west London, England, as an "evening star" in spring 2007.

EARLY OBSERVATIONS

Galileo's simple telescope was enough to reveal that Venus went through a complete set of phases, just like the Moon. He realized that this showed that Venus was in orbit around the Sun, not Earth. Here was clear evidence—though not yet complete proof—that the Sun and not Earth was at the center of the solar system.

"Galileo, with an opera glass, discovered a more splendid series of celestial phenomena than anyone since."

—RALPH WALDO EMERSON

An exquisite pairing between a crescent Moon and Venus shining to its upper right in evening twilight.

An amateur astronomer's photo of Venus, using a CCD camera, shows the planet as a fine crescent in a daylight sky.

VIEWING VENUS

Like Galileo, you can spot the phases of Venus with a small telescope or even binoculars. You will note how much larger it appears as a crescent—when it is closest—than when it resembles a half moon or has a gibbous phase and is much farther away. Disappointingly, because of its blanket of clouds, Venus appears rather bland. Amateur astronomers have sketched shadings and different levels of brightness on Venus's disk that may be caused by real patterns in the clouds. Some observers have reported a faint glow on the night side of the planet when it is in a dark sky. Dubbed "ashen light," its cause is not known, but there are suggestions that it could be lightning or other physical effects within Venus's atmosphere.

WARNING

Never sweep for Venus with binoculars when the Sun is in the sky. You might point them at it and suffer serious eye damage.

TRANSITS OF VENUS

On June 8, 2004, astronomers watched the silhouette of Venus travel gracefully across the face of the Sun. This transit of Venus was the first such event witnessed since 1882. However, transits of Venus occur in pairs, and so there will be another on June 6, 2012. After that, we will have to wait until December 11, 2117.

A RARE ALIGNMENT

Transits of Venus are rare because Venus's orbit around the Sun is slightly inclined, or tilted, by 3 degrees to that of Earth. As a result, when Venus reaches inferior conjunction, it usually appears to pass either above or below the Sun. Transits of Venus can occur only at the points, called nodes, where the planes of the orbits of our two planets intersect in June and December.

Like all planets traveling the path of the ecliptic, Venus may also occasionally be covered by the Moon. Because Venus is so bright, these events—termed occultations—may be observed in daylight.

A BIT OF LUCK

Johannes Kepler predicted transits of the Sun by Venus in the early seventeenth century. In 1639 the 20-year-old British mathematician Jeremiah Horrocks realized that one would occur that December. Horrocks successfully observed the spectacle from his home at Hoole, near Liverpool, by projecting the Sun's disk onto a white sheet of paper through the recently invented telescope. As he commented: "O most gratifying spectacle! . . . I perceived a new spot of unusual magnitude and of a perfectly round form, that had just wholly entered upon the left limb of the Sun." William Crabtree, a fellow mathematician and astronomer, was alerted to the forthcoming event by Horrocks, and he also observed part of the transit.

A fanciful painting imagines how Jeremiah Horrocks might have rigged up a telescope to project the transit of Venus onto a sheet of paper inside his home in England in 1639.

COOK'S TOURS

In the seventeenth century it was realized that measurements during a transit of Venus from different parts of Earth would, by using simple geometry, allow the distance of Earth from the Sun to be determined. For the transit of 1769, Britain's Royal Society dispatched several expeditions, including one led by Captain Cook to Tahiti in the South Pacific. Cook observed the event and added to his success by exploring the east coast of Australia and charting New Zealand.

THE BLACK-DROP EFFECT

The moment when Venus first touches the edge of the Sun during a transit is called first contact; second contact occurs when the planet has moved completely onto the solar disk. Historically, observers reported it difficult to time second contact because Venus's silhouette appeared to cling to the Sun's edge as a black drop. A similar effect was reported just before the moment of third contact, when Venus appears to touch the opposite edge of the Sun. Observations during the first transit of modern times, in 2004, suggest that this is caused by a combination of atmospheric effects, diffraction in the telescope, and the darkening toward the edge of the Sun where its light is less intense.

Sketches by Captain James Cook and Dr. Charles Green record the passage of Venus in front of the Sun on their expedition to the southern hemisphere in 1769.

"I perceived a new spot of unusual magnitude and of a perfectly round form, that had just wholly entered upon the left limb of the Sun."

—JEREMIAH HORROCKS, ASTRONOMER

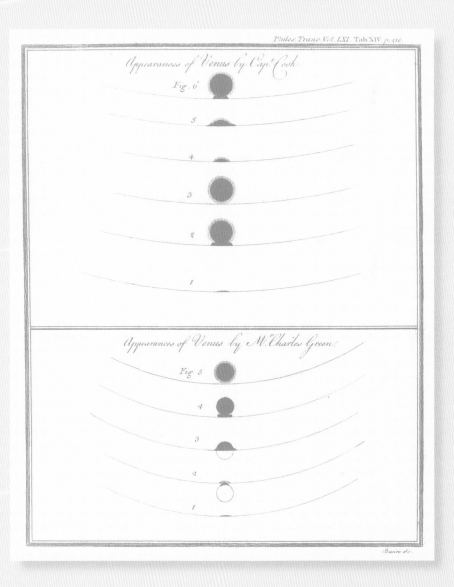

CHAPTER SEVEN

MARS

Mars, the fourth planet from the Sun, comes closer to Earth than any planet except Venus. At its brightest it almost looks like a drop of blood suspended in the heavens—no wonder the planet was identified with gods of war by some ancient peoples. Other civilizations saw Mars as a flaming torch or a burning ember. The distinctive color is caused by the iron oxide in the planet's soil that is similar to rust.

There is a striking difference between the terrain of Mars's northern and southern hemispheres. In the North the landscape is generally flat and smooth, but the South is a dramatic region of rugged highlands with an average height just less than 4 miles (6 km) higher than that of the North. Scientists believe this difference was caused by a massive impact in the North by a body bigger than Pluto at least 3.9 billion years ago. Each of the low plains are called *planitia* and each of the high plains *planum*. Mars may be a lot smaller than Earth, with a diameter of 4,213 miles (6,780 km), but it has surface features that put anything on Earth to shame, including several giant volcanoes, with the biggest in the solar system, Olympus Mons, standing 16 miles (26 km) high. A 2,500-mile (4,000-km) -long gash in the Martian crust called Valles Marineris dwarfs the 280-mile (450-km) -long Grand Canyon. Another giant impact crater forms the Hellas Basin, 1,430 miles (2,300 km) from side to side and more than 5.6 miles (9 km) deep.

"Mars is there, waiting to be reached."

—BUZZ ALDRIN, APOLLO II ASTRONAUT

WHAT WE KNEW THEN

In the late nineteenth century it was generally assumed that Mars was inhabited. The Martians were thought to have built complex irrigation systems that watered the whole planet and allowed vegetation to thrive. There were serious suggestions that we should attempt to contact these beings—and some novel methods were proposed.

WHAT WE THINK WE KNOW NOW

Mars is a cold desert of a planet, though it is clear that many millions of years ago, liquid water must have been plentiful at the surface. Today, vast amounts of water ice are locked underground—as must be any Martians. If life exists, it will be in the form of primitive microbes, not monsters.

A giant dust storm blows up on Mars, a regular occurrence that can hide features on the red planet for months on end.

MARS'S ORBIT

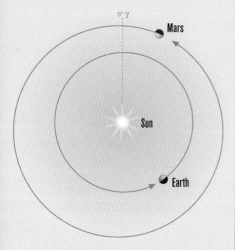

Mars has an eccentric orbit, which means that its distance from Earth varies hugely, even when the two worlds are at their closest.

Mars is a much smaller world than Earth with a diameter a little more than half that of our own planet.

CHANGING VIEWS OF MARS

Mars has a particularly eccentric orbit, and its distance from the Sun ranges from a little more than 128.4 million miles (206 million km) at its closest (perihelion) to nearly 154.9 million miles (250 million km) when at its farthest (aphelion). Mars takes 687 Earth days to orbit the Sun, making a Martian year nearly twice as long as our own.

CLOSE ENCOUNTERS

The distance between Mars and Earth varies enormously, depending on whether we are on the same or opposite side of the Sun. Oppositions of Mars, when the Red Planet is most prominent, occur approximately every 780 days—nearly every 26 months. Because of Mars's eccentric orbit, its distance at opposition varies, too. That of August 2003 was the closest for nearly 60,000 years, with only 35 million miles (56 million km) between us. By December 2007 the gap had widened to 55 million miles (88 million km).

SIZE MATTERS

As Mars's distance changes, its apparent size in the telescope will, too. Astronomers measure this apparent size as an angle, a fraction of a degree. During the year of the record close approach in 2003, Mars grew from just 4 arcseconds to an impressive 25 arcseconds. It managed only 16 arcseconds at the opposition of 2007 and will be even smaller at the oppositions of January 2010 and March 2012. The distances will then gradually increase until Mars swells to a mighty 24 arcseconds in July 2018.

NIGHT AND DAY

In 1610 Galileo was the first to note the gibbous, moonlike phase Mars goes through when we are able to peer a little around its night side. In the mid-seventeenth century the Dutch astronomer Christiaan Huygens made the first sketches of details on Mars, recording a region shaped like India that today we call Syrtis Major. As he watched the feature move as Mars rotated, he estimated the Martian day to be 24 hours long, like that of Earth. In 1666 the Parisian astronomer Giovanni Cassini refined this figure to 24 hours 40 minutes, which is less than 3 minutes out from today's figure of 24 hours 37 minutes 22 seconds. A Martian day is termed a sol.

THE KEY FOR KEPLER

When Tycho Brahe compiled his star catalog in the sixteenth century, he also made precise measurements of the position of Mars over time. His student Johannes Kepler was puzzled because Mars was not where Brahe's orbital calculations suggested it should be. Then he realized why—Mars's orbit was oval and not circular. The discovery helped Kepler formulate his laws of planetary motion.

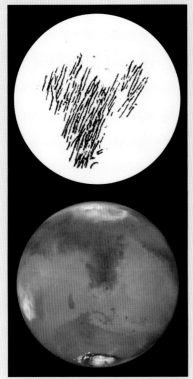

Christiaan Huygens's seventeenth-century sketch of the prominent Syrtis Major feature on Mars compares favorably with the photo beneath it taken with the Hubble Space Telescope.

"I ought not to claim that I can see the phases of Mars. However, unless I am deceiving myself, I believe I have already seen that it is not perfectly round."

—GALILEO GALILEI

POLES APART

Huygens was also first to sketch a Martian polar region, outlining a light zone at the south pole in 1672. Italian scientist Giancomo Miraldi saw white spots at the poles in 1704 and wondered if they might be ice. In 1777 William Herschel agreed they were deep layers of snow and ice. He also saw that the Martian axis was tilted like Earth's and realized that this meant that Mars had seasons. In 1907 naturalist and astronomer Alfred Wallace correctly proposed that the ice caps were made of frozen carbon dioxide.

A global mosaic of Mars built up from satellite images shows the spectacular grand canyon Valles Marineris.

MARKINGS ON MARS

MARKINGS ON MARS

RECORD BREAKER

The wildly different relief of the Martian hemispheres was probably caused by a major asteroid impact around 4 billion years ago. U.S. scientists, using data from orbiting Mars probes, revealed in 2008 that a world the size of Pluto formed the Borealis Basin, which, at 6,600 miles (10,600 km) wide, is the biggest known crater in the solar system.

Eager to exploit the power of the telescope, astronomers tried to see more of Mars. Sketches of dark features and white spots led to the first crude maps, including the illusory canals. High-powered cameras on orbiting spacecraft have now shown us the whole planet in dramatic detail.

VEGETATION OR OCEANS?

As observers sketched the markings on Mars, suggestions as to what they might be included seas, continents, and even clouds. Believers in an oceanic nature named features using nautical terms such as bay, strait, sea, and island—the prominent feature, Syrtis Major, that Huygens drew, has also been known as the Kaiser Sea, the Hourglass Sea, and the Atlantic Canal. Others suggested the markings were a form of vegetation such as lichen. The idea was first put forward by French astronomer Emmanuel Liais in 1860, and the theory persisted well into the twentieth century in works of science fiction.

CANALS CONFUSION

The first detailed map of Mars was produced by the Italian astronomer Giovanni Schiaparelli in 1877. His chart included a network of fine, straight lines, which he labeled *canali*, meaning channels. Schiaparelli believed these channels were carrying water away from the melting ice caps, and he hinted that intelligent aliens might have created them. The idea was picked up by American astronomer Percival Lowell, who built his own observatory at Flagstaff, Arizona. He mapped what he called canals and felt that there was no doubt they were an irrigation network built by advanced beings.

PAINTING BY NUMBERS

In 1964, *Mariner 4*, the first spacecraft to take close-up pictures of Mars, revealed a cratered landscape similar to that of the Moon. NASA scientists were so impatient to see the view that they scribbled out rough sketches on a grid as the data dribbled back in a stream of numbers. By chance, *Mariner 4*'s flight path only carried it over the rugged mountains, so it saw none of the evidence of a water-carved landscape. The breakthrough came in 1972 when *Mariner 9* became the first probe to go into orbit. It was

Percival Lowell made detailed sketches of canals on Mars, but his dark waterways have proved to be entirely illusory.

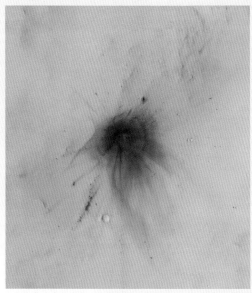

This fresh impact crater, about 75 feet (23 m) wide and surrounded by dark debris, was spotted in Arabia Terra by *Mars Global Surveyor* in 2006.

able to make a global map of Mars that revealed canyons, volcanoes, sand dunes, and features that resembled dried-up riverbeds.

A MASS OF DIFFERENCE

Mars is smaller and only 30 percent less dense than Earth, and its gravity is only 38 percent as strong as ours—which means that the first explorers will feel very light on their feet! Though not a lot is known about the interior of Mars, because of the planet's small size and distance from the Sun, scientists believe the core is largely solid. The crust is estimated to be 30 miles (50 km) deep and mainly composed of the volcanic rock basalt. Space probes have found evidence that there was once movement of the crust, or plate tectonics, similar to that which causes the continents to drift on Earth.

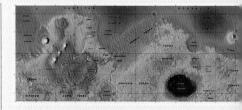

A false-color map of Mars by U.S. geologists indicates the principal regions of the planet.

The channels as mapped by Giovanni Schiaparelli were wrongly believed to be canals by Percival Lowell.

CRATERS PREDICTED

Some astronomers had predicted that there would be impact craters on Mars. Estonian-born Ernst Öpik in the 1920s pointed to the proximity of the asteroid belt. The idea was also proposed by Donald Cyr in 1944 to explain the bloblike "oases" in Mars's canal system —though he also explained the canals as tracks left by nomadic creatures! In 2006 NASA revealed that impacts were still happening at an estimated rate of 12 per year, as evidenced by the 20 new craters recorded by space probes over a seven-year period.

WINDS AND WEATHER

Like Earth, Mars has an atmosphere, but it is more than 95 percent carbon dioxide. Its pinkish color, tinged by particles of high-flying dust, gives photographs from the surface an almost homely feel—contrasting with the bleak, sterile shots from the airless Moon—and sunsets on Mars have a hazy glow.

THIN TIME OF IT

Early astronomers, including Giovanni Cassini, assumed that Mars would have an atmosphere, but it was first scientifically examined by Sir William Herschel. He was viewing on a rare occasion when Mars passed virtually in front of a pair of stars. Neither star dimmed in the slightest, showing that the Martian air must be quite insignificant. Scientific measurements revealed that Mars's atmosphere is 100 times thinner than ours, and the air pressure is only 0.6 percent that of Earth's. Apart from the predominant carbon dioxide, there are tiny amounts of nitrogen, argon, and carbon monoxide, plus a mere hint of oxygen.

The density of the Martian atmosphere can vary, however, and this may be what caused the loss of a British probe, *Beagle 2*, that was due to land on Christmas Day, 2003, after being released from its ESA mothership *Mars Express*. Scientists never heard so much as a yelp from their *Beagle*, and they believe that a dust storm may have left the air thinner than usual, causing the probe to parachute too fast and crash on the surface.

The Mars rover *Spirit* records a spectacular sunset on the Red Planet in May 2005, illuminating dust in the hazy atmosphere.

The Hubble space telescope views a planet-wide dust storm that blew up and engulfed Mars in 2001.

MARTIAN METEORS

An orbiting NASA probe has found signs of shooting stars, or meteors, in the atmosphere of Mars. The flashes themselves were not seen, but the *Mars Global Surveyor* recorded their signatures in disturbances caused in the ionosphere as they vaporized about 50–60 miles (80–95 km) above the surface.

STORMY WEATHER

Early-morning mists are common, but Mars's high-altitude clouds are too insubstantial for rain ever to fall. Despite the atmosphere's low density, the planet can experience dramatic weather. Winds occasionally whip up huge dust storms that can last for months and spread over the entire planet. The effects of the winds can be seen in the sculpted shapes of sand dunes and the weathering of ancient craters. Generally winds blow as a gentle breeze at around 6 miles per hour (10 kmph), though they can gust up to as much as 55 miles per hour (90 kmph).

Cameras on Mars have captured movies of peculiar whirlwinds whipping across the landscape. These dust devils, which can tower more than 5 miles (8 km) high, resemble similar dervishes that dash across deserts here on Earth, and they are caused when sunlight makes the ground hotter than the air above. The lower air is warmed and rises, as plumes of colder air fall in what are termed convection cells. A gust of wind is all it takes to flip these cells on their sides, forming vertical columns that spin ever faster as hot air rises through their centers.

SOLAR POWER

Wind systems are driven by sunshine on Mars just as on Earth. They begin when sunlight heats up lower layers of the atmosphere, the warm air rises, and cooler air floods in to take its place. But generally Mars is a cold place. At the equator temperatures can reach 70°F (20°C) at midday, but the average temperature over the planet is −76°F (−60°C) and drops to −195°F (−125°C) near the poles. Seasonal changes at the poles, with the cyclical formation and evaporation of dry ice, also affect the weather patterns.

NO MAGNETIC PERSONALITY

Unlike Earth, Mars lacks the protective shield of a magnetic field around it. This means that radiation from deep space and from solar flares bombards the surface instead of being deflected around the planet. It also allows the solar wind gradually to strip away the upper atmosphere, helping to keep the air thin.

SPOT MARS

The red planet will be brightest and easiest to see in the months around these dates of opposition:

2010 January 29—Cancer
2012 March 12—Leo
2014 April 8—Virgo
2016 May 22—Scorpius

The *Spirit* rover captures a dust devil whipping its way across the Martian terrain.

FINDING THE WATER

The surface of Mars is arid compared with that of Earth, but this was not always the case. There is overwhelming evidence that the Red Planet was once awash with water—in fact, a blue planet with oceans. Water is the key to life, so scientists want to know what happened to it on Mars.

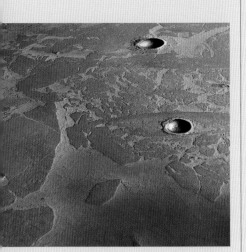

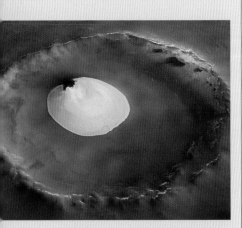

A view of the Elysium region taken from *Mars Express* shows patterning that resembles that of pack ice on Earth.

Water ice is imaged by the *Mars Express* probe in a 20-mile (32-km) -wide crater in the Vastitas Borealis around 70.5 degrees north.

NORTHERN OCEAN

Planetary experts believe that more than 3.8 billion years ago an ocean covered most of Mars's northern hemisphere. Photographs of the southern highlands reveal ancient channels carved by water that flowed toward this sea. *Spirit* and *Opportunity*, two U.S. robot rovers that landed on opposite sides of Mars in 2004, discovered deposits of sulfates and phosphates, which commonly form in water. *Opportunity* also found a crop of what scientists call blueberries—mineral balls produced by water rising through the sediment and left like a dirty ring around a bathtub. However, any ancient seas either evaporated into space or disappeared underground.

GO WITH THE FLOE

Mars's south pole has been the target for water exploration. Space probes, using ground-piercing radar to study the region, have discovered that dry ice (carbon dioxide) at the surface lies on top of vast quantities of water ice over an area greater than Texas. *Mars Express*, which went into orbit in December 2003, measured more than 300 slices using an instrument called MARSIS—the Mars Advanced Radar for

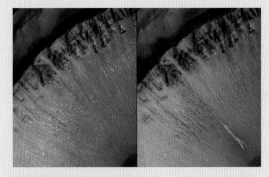

Images that appeared to show evidence of liquid water running down a crater's slope in 2006 turned out to be a false alarm.

Subsurface and Ionospheric Sounding. In 2007 it was reported that enough polar ice had been found to cover the entire planet with water 36 feet (11 m) deep. *Mars Express* also found that there were hundreds of square miles of permafrost—water ice mixed with the soil—surrounding the south pole.

More images from *Mars Express* of a region near the equator called Elysium show features that look remarkably like pack ice beneath the sand. They resemble ice floes, fractures, and ridges reminiscent of frozen regions on Earth. Scientists say they could be evidence of a giant frozen lake the size of the North Sea in Europe. This region is a prime target for future landers to explore in the search for signs of microbial life.

Sand dunes fill the half-mile-wide Victoria Crater in a photo from NASA's *Mars Reconnaissance Orbiter*. The crater in Meridiani Planum was explored by the rover *Opportunity*.

Lumps of ice appear in the shaded area of a trench scooped out by *Phoenix*. The brighter patches may be mineral salts.

THE WHIFF OF WATER

There could be no doubt that Mars harbored water, and scientists finally got to touch and sniff it following the arrival of NASA's *Phoenix* lander in May 2008. *Phoenix*, which touched down gently in a region of permafrost, 68 degrees north, called Vastitas Borealis, took a scoop of Martian soil that appeared to contain balls of ice. A few days later that ice had vanished!

NASA followed up by warming some soil in an oven aboard *Phoenix*. The vapor released carried the unmistakable signature of water. The water find came two years after a false alarm when NASA thought they had photographed liquid water flowing down crater walls. They turned out to be landslides. Scientists have suggested that the soil on Mars might be suitable for growing crops such as asparagus.

ERUPTING GEYSERS

Scientists were puzzled by mysterious dark spots that appeared around the south polar ice cap every Martian spring. Having studied images taken by *Mars Odyssey*, they now understand that these are left by violent eruptions of carbon dioxide gas as the ice cap warms. The geysers carry dark sand and dust high into the sky before it falls back to the surface, proving that this region of Mars is still dynamically active.

VAPOR IN THE AIR

In 1894 American astronomer William Wallace Campbell used a spectroscope to look for water in the Martian atmosphere but failed to find any. Traces of water vapor have since been detected but so little that, if it all condensed, it would create a layer over the planet just 0.0004 inch (10 micrometers) thick. By contrast, there is sufficient water vapor in Earth's atmosphere to lie just over three-quarters of an inch (2 cm) deep.

An artist imagines the view as geysers erupt near the Martian south pole with the coming of spring.

THE QUEST FOR LIFE

We have long been fascinated by the idea that Mars is inhabited. Before there was any evidence either way, it seemed natural to assume that other worlds had their own civilizations. Mars's similarities to Earth still make it a possible candidate for life, albeit in simple and primitive forms—and the search is on.

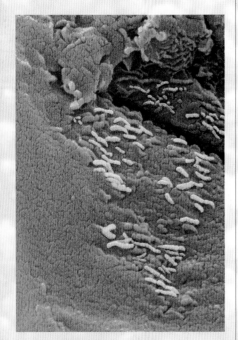

The notion of life on Mars inspired science-fiction classics such as H. G. Wells's *The War of the Worlds*, which has been translated to the cinema.

The tiny "fossils" found in the Mars meteorite are less than a hundredth the width of a human hair.

MAGIC OF THE MARTIANS

The idea of canals irrigating Mars may have been proven incorrect, but it certainly fed the fertile imaginations of science-fiction writers. Mars was the home of the invaders in H. G. Wells's classic *The War of the Worlds*, and many other writers—including Tarzan creator Edgar Rice Burroughs, C. S. Lewis, and Ray Bradbury—were inspired to set their own adventures on the Red Planet. A lurid set of bubblegum cards from the early 1960s inspired Tim Burton's spoof B-movie *Mars Attacks!* more than 40 years later, and musician David Bowie asked whether there is "Life on Mars?".

ALL DONE WITH MIRRORS

A nineteenth-century French inventor, Charles Cros, suggested letting Martians know we were here by building a giant mirror to focus sunlight and burn messages into the planet's sands. Other suggestions included communicating with the aliens by planting patterns of trees in Siberia, digging a circular ditch in the Sahara and filling it with burning kerosene, or setting up a network of mirrors in European cities to shine like the stars of the Big Dipper.

Fantasy aside, many scientists believe that Mars could have been home to life in the past, and may still be now. It has the essential ingredients: carbon and other chemical elements, water, and energy, such as sunlight or heat, from the planet's interior. On the downside, Mars is bombarded by radiation, but some think Martians could be shielded beneath the planet's thick, icy crust. The idea is not so preposterous as it seems—simple life forms known as extremophiles have been discovered on Earth in such hostile environments as boiling, toxic vents on the ocean floor and in radioactive chambers, and micro-organisms have been revived after being brought up from 2 miles (3 km) beneath the Antarctic ice.

DIGGING FOR THE FACTS

If the Martians really are underground, this explains why they have not yet been found. Early landers have barely scratched the surface, but NASA's *Phoenix* dug into the soil on Mars after its arrival in May 2008, and a European robot called ExoMars will drill down more than 6 feet (2 m) when it lands in 2015. Some scientists have made the controversial claim that two Viking landers in 1976 may have detected the presence of microbes, but unwittingly drowned or baked them alive.

MYSTERY OF THE METEORITE

Chunks of Mars have been found lying on Earth, having been blasted out of the planet and crashing here after eons spent circling the Sun. One of these meteorites, found in the Antarctic, hit the headlines in 1996 when NASA announced it contained the fossils of wormlike alien microbes. The news was splashed across the world's newspapers, and U.S. President Bill Clinton addressed the nation. Sadly, scientists today are highly skeptical and believe the meteorite was contaminated by more down-to-earth bacteria.

THE FACE ON MARS

Scientists have hoped to find life, but they never expected to see a Martian staring back at them. An image from the *Viking 1* orbiter in 1976 clearly showed what appeared to be a human face. NASA released the picture for fun, even though they knew it was a trick of the light on a hill in a region called Cydonia. Rational explanations did not deter some, however, who decided aliens were trying to contact us and went on to find other imaginary features, even a ruined city. Detailed close-ups from later probes confirm they are illusions—just like those canals.

The *Viking 1* orbiter's image of a "face" staring into space (below left) was clearly shown by the *Mars Express* probe to be a natural rock feature (below)

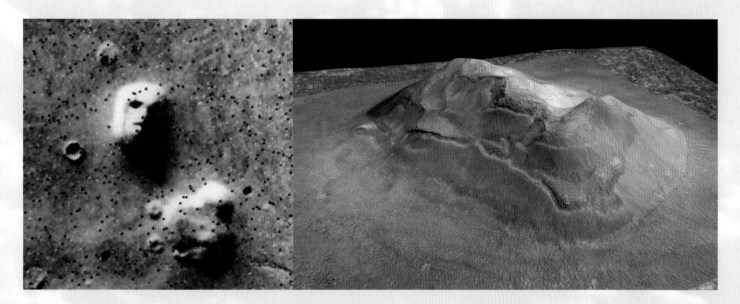

"But who shall dwell in these worlds if they be inhabited? . . .
Are we or they Lords of the World?"

—JOHANNES KEPLER, QUOTED ON THE TITLE PAGE OF
"THE WAR OF THE WORLDS," BY H. G. WELLS

THE MARTIAN SATELLITES

Mars has two moons, Phobos and Deimos, but they are tiny, insignificant worlds compared with our Moon. Irregular-shaped and pockmarked with craters, they appear to be chunks of the same rocks that built the planets, captured from the asteroid belt by Mars's gravitational pull.

Phobos is revealed to be a rocky body like an asteroid in this photo of the moon taken from NASA's *Mars Reconnaissance Orbiter* in 2008.

The shadow of Phobos is photographed on the martian surface from orbit by the *Mars Global Surveyor* in August 1999.

TWO MOONS

Mars was thought to have two moons before even one had actually been discovered. They were predicted by the Irish satirical writer Jonathan Swift in his classic *Gulliver's Travels* in 1726. Perhaps he was emulating Johannes Kepler, who had proposed, without any scientific basis, that if Venus had no moons and Earth had one, then there must be two around Mars. The French philosopher Voltaire also wrote a story called "Micromégas" suggesting a similar number.

FEAR AND PANIC

The two moons were first spotted in 1877 by the astronomer Asaph Hall of the U.S. Naval Observatory in Washington, D.C. Hall sought them out using what was then one of the world's largest telescopes, which had a giant 26-inch (66-cm) objective lens—they would be visible in smaller telescopes if it were not for the glare of Mars itself. As their discoverer, Hall took the advice of Henry Madan, a teacher at the leading English private school Eton, and called the moons Phobos (meaning fear) and Deimos (meaning panic). These were the names of the sons of Mars, the Greek god of war.

PHOBOS

Though Phobos is the larger satellite, it is still only 17 miles (27 km) across at its widest. Its most notable feature, first spotted by the *Viking 1* orbiter in 1978, is a crater so big that the impact must almost have broken Phobos in two. Called Stickney—the maiden name of Hall's wife, Chloe—the crater is about 5.5 miles (9 km) in diameter. Phobos is also crossed by a series of grooves that were first thought to be associated with the impact. *Mars Express* scientists now believe, however, that these were gouged out by ejected debris from an asteroid strike on Mars itself.

Phobos is so small that it has a very weak gravitational pull. This has prompted scientists to propose using it as a testing ground for bringing back samples to Earth. Landing might be tricky, but it would be much easier to take off from Phobos than from Mars itself. Russia

ORBIT OF DOOM

Phobos, which the rover *Opportunity* has photographed several times crossing the face of the Sun in a Martian eclipse, is doomed either to collide with Mars or break up into rings in about 11 million years' time.

plans to launch such a sample-return mission in 2009, and the ESA is considering a similar mission in the following decade.

Phobos is unusually close to Mars, with a circular orbit that carries it just 2,300 miles (3,700 km) above the surface. It zips around the planet in 7 hours 39 minutes, so a Martian month measured by Phobos is around a third the length of a sol (a Martian day). Oddly, a rapid orbit was also conceived by Jonathan Swift.

Phobos's giant impact crater Stickney contains a smaller crater, shown in this close-up taken from the MRO probe.

DEIMOS

Mars's second moon, Deimos, is only 9 miles (15 km) at its widest, and it orbits farther out, circling the planet once every 30 hours 18 minutes at a height of 7,800 miles (12,500 km) above the Martian surface. Unlike Phobos, it would appear to rise in the east and spend nearly three days in the sky before setting. Deimos has a smoother surface than Phobos, but two craters, each measuring roughly 2 miles (3 km) wide, have been named after those imaginative writers Swift and Voltaire.

The rover *Opportunity* caught Phobos passing directly in front of the Sun in March 2004.

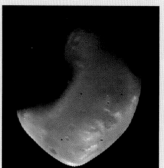

Deimos, a smaller and smoother asteroid-like body, pictured from the *Viking 1* orbiter in 1977.

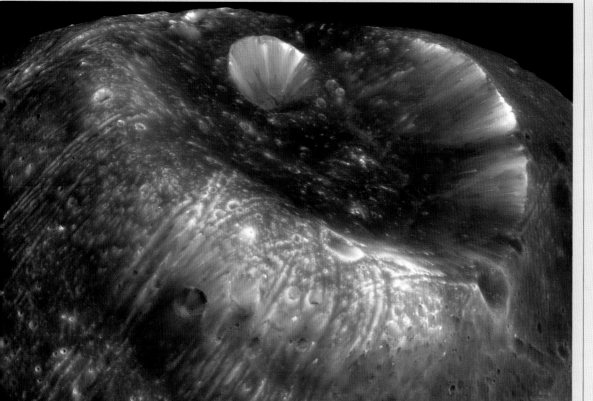

CHAPTER EIGHT

JUPITER

Jupiter is the unchallenged King of the Planets and the largest body in the solar system after the Sun. Early people must have had a suspicion about its special ranking, since it was named after the supreme deity in the Roman pantheon. They probably noted that, while Venus and occasionally Mars can become brighter, Jupiter is constant in shining boldly in the heavens, apart from a few months when it lies on the other side of the Sun. It can dominate a dark night sky at magnitude −2.8 and, unlike Venus, is visible throughout the night when near opposition.

Jupiter is more than 2.5 times as massive as all the other planets put together, and it could contain more than 1,300 Earths. But it is quite a different planet from the terrestrial worlds. Often labeled a gas giant, it has no solid surface, unlike our rocky Earth. The features we see on Jupiter are the colorful belts and swirls in its cloud tops, including one storm—the Great Red Spot—that has been seen to rage for hundreds of years. Jupiter's immense size makes it a force to be reckoned with, and it has exerted a major influence on the orbits of other bodies. It is also at the center of its own kind of mini-solar system, with four large moons and at least 59 other smaller bodies in orbit around it.

"Only this evening I have seen Jupiter accompanied by three fixed stars."

—GALILEO GALILEI,
ON FIRST SEEING THREE OF JUPITER'S MOONS

WHAT WE KNEW THEN

Isaac Newton's theory of universal gravitation, published in 1687, helped astronomers understand the attraction that physical bodies have for each other. It became clear that though Jupiter is a mighty world in size, it is not massive enough to be solid like the Earth and was unlikely to have a solid surface.

WHAT WE THINK WE KNOW NOW

The Hubble telescope and supporting observations of two giant storms erupting on Jupiter in 2007 showed that such tempests are triggered deep down in water clouds by hot jets that send ammonia ice racing at 375 miles per hour (600 kmph) high above the visible cloud layer.

Giant planet Jupiter looms over the horizon of Europa, an icy Galilean moon that could be hiding a warm ocean beneath it surface.

OBSERVING A GIANT

Jupiter is so big that it shows as a disk even through a small telescope. It therefore attracted attention soon after the instrument was invented. Anyone pointing a telescope at the planet must have noticed immediately that it was attended by some bright companions—its family of moons—almost like a mini-solar system.

THE BIG FOUR

Steadily held binoculars will reveal Jupiter's four Galilean satellites. But they should, theoretically, be bright enough to be visible to the naked eye, were it not for the overpowering glare of their parent planet. Indeed, a Chinese astrologer, Gan De, is said to have spotted one of them—probably the brightest, Ganymede—way back in the fourth century B.C.

A STRING OF BEADS

Four of Jupiter's satellites—Io, Europa, Ganymede, and Callisto—are big enough to be seen easily, spread out on either side of the planet like a string of beads. Galileo noticed them right away early in 1610 but first mistook them for "three little stars"—presumably the fourth was out of sight. He was puzzled at first when these "stars" appeared to remain close to Jupiter while moving from one side to the other. Finally he recognized that they were orbiting the planet, and they became known as the Galilean satellites. The discovery was of huge importance because it showed that not everything in the sky orbited Earth, as had been imagined.

NAMING AND SHAMING

The names of the four main satellites were chosen by the German astronomer Simon Marius, who owned his own telescope and claimed to have spotted them a few weeks before Galileo. Unfortunately for Marius, he failed to publish his observations, so the credit rightly went to Galileo, who rebuked Marius in writing for his statement. Galileo had wanted to name the satellites after those patrons who supported his work financially, but Marius eventually prevailed with the names that were suggested to him in 1613 by none other than Johannes Kepler. Even so, the names were not officially recognized until well into the twentieth century after the formation of the IAU.

Galileo kept a record of his sketches of the positions of Jupiter's moons in his work *Siderius Nuncius*.

JUPITER'S WEATHER PATTERNS

North Polar Region

North North Temperate Zone

North North Temperate Belt

North Temperate Zone

North Temperate Belt

North Tropical Zone

North Equatorial Belt

Equatorial Zone

South Equatorial Belt

South Tropical Zone

South Temperate Belt

South Temperate Zone

South South Temperate Belt

South South Temperate Zone

South Polar Region

Jupiter's weather patterns form several bands as shown in this photo of the planet (the "zones" are bright and the "belts" are generally dark). The Great Red Spot is also visible.

SKETCH SHOW

Coordinated observations of Jupiter by amateur astronomers began during the nineteenth century on both sides of the Atlantic. Because of Jupiter's rapid rotation, observers would quickly sketch the features they saw. They would also time the moment when prominent markings crossed the center of the disk in order to help gauge the length of Jupiter's day. Different belts and bands were given names, such as the North Temperate Belt and the South Tropical Zone. Winds blow in opposite directions in the dark belts (east to west) and bright zones (west to east). Their boundaries are often far from distinct. The observation work of amateurs greatly aided professional astronomers, because the blurring caused by Earth's atmosphere made photography difficult. Sketches of Jupiter are still made today, though special digital cameras and processing techniques are allowing amateurs to take splendidly detailed photographs of the planet.

HIDE AND SEEK

Every six years or so, celestial alignments allow us to see the plane of Jupiter's satellites' orbits edge-on. Then for about 18 months, we have the chance to observe the Galilean moons occult or eclipse each other. An occultation occurs when one satellite passes in front of another. An eclipse occurs when one moon enters the shadow of another. In the eighteenth century, these observations of eclipses published in the *Philosophical Transactions* of the Royal Society in London. The next sequence of these so-called mutual events will take place in 2009–10.

Jupiter's chariot, decorated with two signs of the zodiac, is set to ride across the heavens in an image from mythology.

BELTS, CLOUDS, AND SPOTS

After Mars, and beyond a gap filled with fragments of rock called asteroids, Jupiter represents the first of an entirely different type of planet from those we have checked out so far. Its chemical makeup and the lack of a solid surface mean that it is sometimes thought to be more like a star that failed to generate the energy to shine.

The *Cassini* space probe took this picture of Jupiter as it flew past the planet en route for Saturn in 2000. The black spot is the shadow of the moon Io, which can itself be seen to its lower right.

HEAVY GOING

Jupiter's gravity at the surface is around 2.4 times stronger than on Earth, which means you would weigh nearly two and a half times as much there as on Earth!

SUPERSIZE ME

Though Jupiter appears huge among the other planets, it is truly cut down to size when compared with the Sun, which could contain a thousand Jupiters. The King of the Planets, which formed in the cooler outer reaches of the solar system, radiates twice as much heat as it receives from the Sun, but it would need to have been about 80 times more massive for the thermonuclear reactions to have kicked in to make it a real star!

UNDER PRESSURE

Despite its vast size, Jupiter weighs only as much as 318 Earths because its composition is much less dense than those of the rocky planets. Its outer layers are made up mainly of hydrogen and helium gases at a cool -166°F (-110°C). Deeper into the clouds the gas becomes much more compressed, like liquid, and temperatures rapidly begin to climb. At a depth of 9,300 miles (15,000 km), it soars above 9,000°F (5,000°C), and the gas behaves more like molten metal. Only at the very heart of Jupiter do we find a truly solid, rocky core, about 12,400 miles (20,000 km) wide.

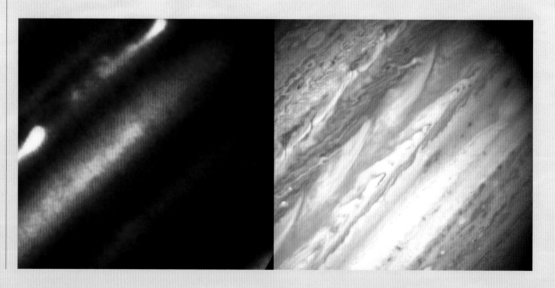

Two views of the same area of Jupiter captured in different wavelengths using the Hubble space telescope in 2007. An infrared image, left, maps the heat given off by the planet, while the right is a view in visible light.

LITTLE BELTER

Jupiter appears a dullish yellow at first glance through a small telescope, but closer inspection reveals it to be crossed by streaks. Larger instruments show that this ball of gas is circled by a system of bright and dark bands of various shades and colors, where winds blow at hundreds of miles per hour. These are the belts of Jupiter, and their cloud tops display a constantly changing pattern that has long fascinated astronomers. They indicate a complex weather system of swirling gases, including methane, ammonia, and water. Recent infrared images taken by the Hubble space telescope tell us that Jupiter's storms are driven by heat from within the planet. Passing space probes and Hubble have revealed Jupiter's belts in great detail, but even amateur astronomers are today taking spectacular photographs, thanks to modern processing techniques that eliminate the blurring caused by our atmosphere.

IN A SPIN

Jupiter rotates more quickly than any other planet, with a day lasting around 9 hours 50 minutes. This rapid spin causes it to bulge markedly at the equator, where the diameter is nearly 88,900 miles (143,000 km), compared with just 83,080 miles (133,700 km) at the poles. The earliest assiduous observers with powerful telescopes noticed that Jupiter's clouds rotate more quickly at the equator than nearer the poles, where a day lasts up to 5 minutes longer.

A PERFECT STORM

Jupiter's most famous feature is a huge storm that has been raging since at least 1831 and shows no sign of blowing out. Called the Great Red Spot, this twisting vortex—twice as wide as the Earth and resembling a giant eye staring back at us—was probably the resurfacing of an even older feature first recorded by the astronomer Cassini in 1665. Before *Voyager 1* sent back the first dramatic close-ups in 1979, some wondered whether it might be a solid or liquid feature. Its edge is rotating at around 225 miles per hour (360 kmph).

Jupiter's visible cloud layer is thought to be only about 30 miles (50 km) deep and driven by convection currents. As well as the waves and swirls, there also appear other small oval spots, often white or brown. In 2005 astronomers watched as one white spot darkened to red until it began to resemble a smaller Great Red Spot, and it was nicknamed Red Jr.

An early eighteenth-century painting by Italian artist Donato Creti shows a hugely magnified view of Jupiter and its main moons, as if seen through a telescope.

SPOT JUPITER

These are opposition dates for Jupiter when it is visible all night. The planet moves steadily from the southern zodiac to its northern constellations:

2009 August 14—Capricornus
2010 September 21—Pisces
2011 October 29—Aries
2012 December 3—Taurus
2014 January 5—Gemini
2015 February 6—Cancer

Our first close-up views of Jupiter, taken from *Voyager 1* in 1979, such as this picture of the Great Red Spot and swirling cloud forms, resembled modern art.

THE MAJOR MOONS

The four main Galilean moons travel in roughly circular orbits, and it is fascinating to watch the changing patterns they make as they fly around Jupiter. They appear simply as points of light when viewed in a small telescope, but in reality each has a very different character from any of the others.

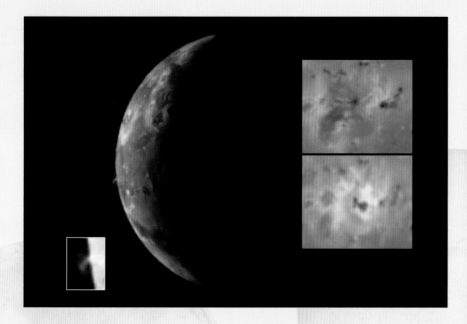

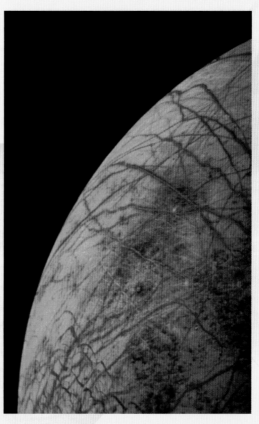

Volcanic activity constantly modifies Io's surface, the heat being generated by Jupiter's powerful tidal pull. These eruptions were captured by the orbiting *Galileo* probe. Right: A close-up of the cracks on Europa taken from *Voyager 2*.

EXPLOSIVE IO

Io, 2,256 miles (3,630 km) in diameter, is the innermost of the main moons, at a distance of 263,000 miles (421,800 km) from Jupiter. Io orbits Jupiter in 1.77 days. It is the most volcanically active world in the solar system. Close-up photographs from the *Galileo* space probe led to its being compared to an exotic pizza, though its constantly replenished and colorful topping is unappetizing molten sulfur and similar compounds. Io always keeps the same face toward Jupiter, whose massive tidal pull causes its surface to bulge in and out by up to 330 feet (100 m). One ton (just over 1,000 kg) of material from Io's surface is being stripped away every second by Jupiter's magnetic field, a process that powers the planet's aurorae.

CRACKING EUROPA

Europa, at 1,950 miles (3,140 km) in diameter, is the smallest of the Galilean satellites—and it could not be more different from Io. A rocky world, which also keeps the same side facing Jupiter, it appears covered by an ocean that is completely frozen over. This icy surface displays an fantastic pattern of cracks, probably caused by the immense tidal pull that is exerted by the giant planet. Scientists are excited by the possibility that these forces are warming a liquid ocean beneath the ice, which could be a prime site in the search for simple alien life. European and American scientists are pressing for a special robotic mission to explore this amazing moon. Europa lies 417,000 miles (671,100 km) from Jupiter, which it orbits in 3.55 days.

GROOVY GANYMEDE

Ganymede, with a diameter of 3,280 miles (5,262 km), has the distinction of being the biggest moon in the solar system—bigger even than Mercury and Pluto. It is thought to have a rocky core surrounded by water ice and a crust of ice and rock. This icy surface has broad, dark, cratered regions that are divided by areas of ridges and grooves, which are also dotted with craters. Ganymede has its own magnetic field, possibly generated by liquid within its interior. The moon lies 664,900 miles (1.07 million km) from Jupiter and circles it once every 7.16 days.

ANCIENT CALLISTO

Callisto, the outermost of the main satellites, is the third largest moon in the solar system, with a diameter of more than 2,980 miles (4,800 km). It also has the oldest terrain in the solar system. It is thought to have a similar make-up to Ganymede but with a smaller rocky core surrounded by ice. The surface is heavily cratered and has remained essentially unchanged in four billion years, thanks to the lack of any geological activity. Lying 1.17 million miles (1.88 million km) from Jupiter, Callisto makes one orbit in a leisurely 16.69 days.

CRASH COURSE

Four U.S. space probes—*Pioneers 10 and 11* and *Voyagers 1* and *2*—flew past Jupiter in the 1970s on their tours of the solar system, and they gave us close-up views of the planet and its moons. Three more—*Ulysses, Cassini-Huygens,* and *New Horizons*—have zoomed by on other missions. But the first dedicated probe to go into orbit around Jupiter, in December 1995, was NASA's *Galileo*. It fired a probe into the clouds and radioed back a wealth of data and pictures over eight years before finally being made to crash into the planet to avoid any chance of hitting and contaminating Europa.

JUNO WHAT?

NASA is sending another spacecraft to orbit Jupiter and continue *Galileo*'s fine work. Solar-powered *Juno* is due to launch in 2011 on a five-year journey. After arriving in 2016, it will probe deep into the planet's atmosphere.

THE GALILEAN SATELLITES

Io

Europa

Ganymede

Callisto

CAPTURED COMPANIONS

Jupiter is circled by many other attendants, all much smaller than the four big moons first observed by Galileo. It also has its own dim ring system, discovered late in the twentieth century, plus an invisible but powerful magnetic field that stretches deep into space.

A cutaway view of Jupiter's rings showing their position in relation to the small inner satellites whose dust has formed them.

❶ Gossamer Rings

❷ Main Ring

❸ Halo

❹ Amalthea

❺ Adrastea

❻ Metis

❼ Thebe

COMET CRASH

A spectacular event was witnessed in 1994 when 21 fragments of Comet Shoemaker-Levy 9 smashed into the clouds of Jupiter. The comet, discovered a year earlier, had been pulled into orbit around the planet. As telescopes on Earth and in space watched, the impacts gave Jupiter a string of "black eyes" that left scars for several months.

SMALL SATELLITES

Amalthea is the biggest of Jupiter's lesser moons, at only 104 miles (168 km) wide. Its tiny size meant that, as the fifth Jovian satellite to be discovered, it was not spotted until 1892. By 1979—the year that *Voyager 1* flew past Jupiter—the number had climbed to 16. The early years of the twenty-first century have seen this figure rocket to 63, thanks to more powerful search techniques—though 47 of the moons are less than 6 miles (10 km) across. No doubt most (if not all) are asteroids that were swept up and captured by Jupiter's gravitational pull.

Jupiter is also encircled by a ring of dust, a fact that was not realized until *Voyager 1* passed by in 1979. Far less complex than neighbor Saturn's dazzling ring system, it is in three parts, the main section being 4,350 miles (7,000 km) wide. Two tiny moons, Adrastea and Metis, orbit Jupiter within this ring system and are the source of the incredibly fine dust that makes up the main ring. The inner, thickest part of the ring is called the halo, while the outer section, the gossamer rings, is fed by dust from Thebe and Amalthea.

LIGHT WORK

The Galilean satellites played an important role in efforts to measure the speed of light. Middle-eastern scientists in the eleventh century had decided that light traveled at a fixed velocity, and Galileo made a crude stab at measuring it with experiments on Earth. Then, in 1675, Danish astronomer Ole Rømer noticed that eclipses of Jupiter's moons were occurring later or earlier than predicted, depending on how far Jupiter was from Earth. He realized this was because it was taking light different lengths of time to travel from the moons to Earth. Rømer's figure of 124,300 miles per second (200,000 km/second) is wrong because distances in the solar system were not correctly known. The true speed of light in a vacuum is about 186,282 miles per second (299,792 km/second).

GIANT MAGNET

Jupiter has a powerful magnetic field, many times stronger than the Earth's. It stretches out like a tail more than 400 million miles (650 million km)—even beyond the orbit of the next planet, Saturn! In February 2007 the *New Horizons* probe rode through this tail as it sped toward its own target, Pluto; it also spotted lightning storms near Jupiter's poles. Jupiter's

magnetosphere causes bright aurorae around its magnetic poles, just like on Earth, and they were imaged in the late 1990s by the Hubble space telescope.

RADIO JUPITER

In 1955 scientists Bernard Burke and Kenneth Franklin were observing the remnant of an exploding star called the Crab Nebula, when their radio telescope—based near Washington, D.C., and which resembled a field full of beanpoles—picked up some unexpected interference. As they collected more data, they realized that the noise was occurring 4 minutes earlier each night—and it was coming from Jupiter. It was the first time any planet had been found to be broadcasting like a radio station. The noise was largely generated by physical interaction with Jupiter's powerful magnetic field.

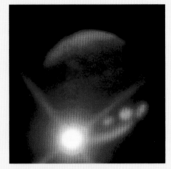

A heat-seeking infrared telescope on Mount Stromlo, Australia, captures the blast as a fragment of Comet Shoemaker-Levy 9 collides with Jupiter in 1994.

Jupiter's aurora are wrapped like sheets around its north magnetic pole in this photo taken in ultraviolet light with the Hubble space telescope.

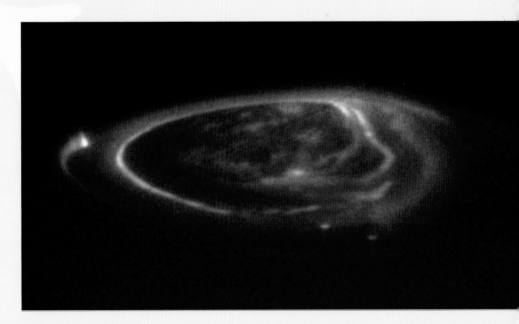

CHAPTER NINE

SATURN

If Jupiter is King of the Planets, then Saturn must be Lord of the Rings. The second largest planet—sixth in order from the Sun—is surely the most stunning object in the night sky visible through a telescope thanks to the brilliant rings that encircle it. A gas world like Jupiter, Saturn is a bright planet that was spotted early in human history because it shines with a steady straw-yellow glow of magnitude -0.3 that sets it above almost all stars. Like Jupiter, Saturn can be seen all night when it is near opposition, and it will dramatically change the appearance of constellations it visits as it makes its 26-year journey around the Sun.

Even through binoculars it becomes clear that there is something very odd about Saturn's shape, and a small telescope will reveal the reason why—those famous rings. Two are clearly visible with a gap between them that can be perceived with a decent amateur telescope. Like Jupiter, Saturn is also attended by a retinue of satellites, including Titan, an orb that intrigues scientists because it resembles a young Earth on which life could evolve.

WHAT WE KNEW THEN

Saturn was the seventh of the wandering bodies in the heavens known to ancient man. They imagined another round and perfect world, in keeping with their notion of celestial perfection. What a shock, then, when Galileo turned his telescope on Saturn and saw that it looked unlike any other planet.

WHAT WE THINK WE KNOW NOW

The true nature of Saturn's rings was revealed only when we traveled out to visit them. In 1980 and 1981, NASA's Voyager space probes discovered that the system was more complex than anyone had imagined, with countless separate rings in intricate patterns made up of myriad particles of rock and ice.

"I have discovered another very strange wonder. . . Saturn is not a single star but a composite of three."

—GALILEO GALILEI

A space probe catches a view of Saturn from the unlit side of the famous rings, their shadows cast across the planet's cloud tops.

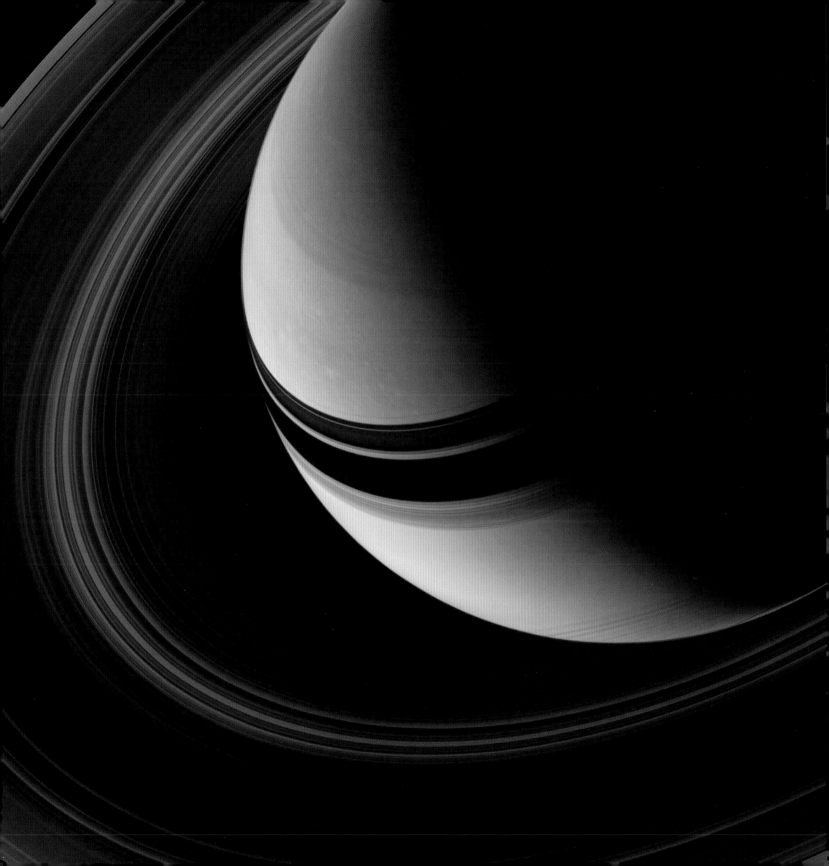

RINGED WONDER

When Galileo turned his telescope on Saturn in 1610, he immediately noticed its unusual shape. However, it did not occur to him that he was seeing a disk of rings around its equator. Instead, he thought the planet was made up of three globes—a large central one and two others, each a third the size, that resembled the handles of a jug.

The moon Tethys can be seen beyond the rings that cast their shadow on Saturn's clouds, in this view taken from the *Cassini* orbiter.

THE TRIPLE PLANET

Galileo thought Saturn's two smaller orbs were somehow fixed, since they did not appear to move or change as he viewed them. As on previous occasions, Galileo wrote up his latest find in the form of an anagram. It is not that scientists of the day were particularly fond of word games; rather, this was an ingenious way of disguising a discovery, preventing others from claiming it as their own until he was able to have it properly published. When unraveled, the anagram stated in Latin, "*Altissimum planetam tergeminum observavi*"—meaning "I have observed the highest planet tri-form."

RINGING THE CHANGES

Having notched up yet another major discovery thanks to his trusty telescope, Galileo received a shock in 1612 when he found that Saturn's two companions had vanished. In Roman mythology the god Saturn ate his offspring to prevent them from deposing him; so Galileo wondered, "Has Saturn swallowed his children?" By chance, he was viewing during a rare period when Saturn's rings were aligned so that they appeared edge-on from Earth, rendering them invisible. Four years later Galileo found that they looked different again, describing them as "two half ellipses with two little dark triangles in the middle." Again, this was because of the changing orientation of the rings.

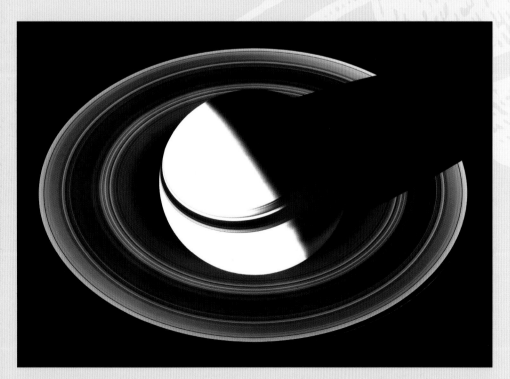

Saturn's own shadow cuts across the rings in this dramatic picture taken from *Cassini*, when the probe flew high above the planet.

A page from Christiaan Huygens's book Systema Saturnium *in which he correctly identified the true nature of Saturn's "handles."*

COMPACT DISK

The Dutch astronomer Christiaan Huygens also studied Saturn from 1655, using a telescope with twice the magnifying power of Galileo's. It was Huygens who hit on the fact that Saturn's "handles" were actually a ring, which he revealed in 1659 in his book *Systema Saturnium*—having previously protected his discovery in a word puzzle, of course. Huygens also observed the shadow of the rings on Saturn and correctly showed that the rings did not actually touch the planet. However, he mistakenly believed the disk of rings to be solid.

GAPS IN KNOWLEDGE

Giovanni Cassini first noticed a gap in the rings in 1675, and this became known as the Cassini Division. Further studies revealed that this 3,000-mile (4,800-km) gap was caused by a shepherding of the particles within the rings by one of Saturn's larger moons, Mimas. Another fainter division, 200 miles (325 km) wide, was found in the outer ring by James Keeler in 1888 and is now dubbed the Encke Gap. It is caused by a small moon, Pan, that orbits inside it. Other small gaps were later discerned, but no one was prepared for the first close-up photos from the Voyager probes in 1980 and 1981, which revealed that there are innumerable rings, all made up of a countless number of fragments of pulverized rock and ice.

PLANE SAILING

Saturn, together with its system of rings, is tilted by 27 degrees to the plane of its orbit around the Sun. The rings would look circular if viewed from above one of the planet's poles. However, because of the tilt, they seem to open and close at different stages of Saturn's orbit. The highly reflective rings are so thin that they can appear to vanish completely every 15 or years so, as Galileo found; this will next take place in 2011. The rings will then begin opening until they are at their widest again in 2018.

SWARM OF MOONLETS

With remarkable foresight, in 1660 the French astronomer Jean Chapelain suggested that Saturn's rings were actually a swarm of tiny satellites—a model that was finally shown to be correct in 1858 by Scottish scientist James Clerk Maxwell.

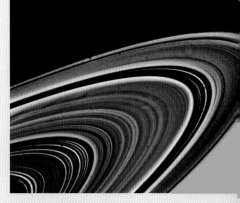

False color is used to highlight the myriad rings in this picture taken during *Voyager 2*'s flyby in 1981.

WINDY WORLD

A SQUASHED WORLD

Saturn's rapid spin, with a day lasting a little more than 10.5 hours, means that, like Jupiter, it bulges at the equator. The diameter there is 74,900 miles (120,540 km) but only 67,560 miles (108,730 km) from pole to pole.

Saturn is nearly half as dense as its big brother Jupiter and is the only planet that is less dense than water—if you could find a big enough tub, it would float! Though it could hold more than 760 Earths, it weighs only 80 times as much as our own planet. Winds blow much faster than on Jupiter, reaching speeds of up to 1,120 miles per hour (1,800 kmph).

BLAND OF GOLD

Compared to the magnificence of its rings, Saturn itself appears rather nondescript. The variations in the colors of its yellowish cloud tops are far more subtle than the swirling patterns within Jupiter's belts. The clouds are three-quarters hydrogen and one-quarter helium, with small amounts of water, methane, and ammonia, too. Like Jupiter, Saturn has no solid surface, but is thought to have a small rocky core at its heart.

A long-lived electrical storm recorded by the *Cassini* probe in March 2008. The left photo shows it in normal colors while the right image is enhanced and sharpened to show the storm more clearly.

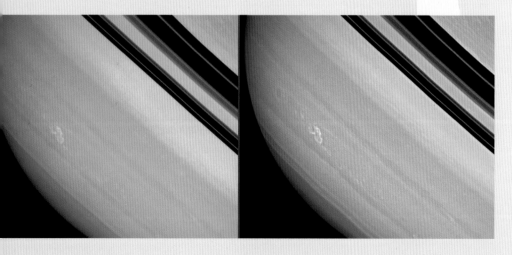

STORM ALLEY

While Saturn lacks any feature as dramatic as Jupiter's Great Red Spot, it does occasionally break out in blemishes of its own. Several white spots have been recorded over the years, which are believed to be huge storms blown up from deep within the clouds. One famous example was first noticed in 1933 by Will Hay, a British amateur astronomer better known for his starring roles in comic movies of the 1930s and '40s, such as *Oh, Mr Porter!* and *Where's That Fire?* An earlier white spot, seen by American astronomer Asaph Hall in 1876, allowed him to measure the time it took Saturn to rotate. The white spots seen by Hall and Hay may be examples of an event on Saturn that recurs every 28 to 30 years, when the northern hemisphere is tilted toward the Sun and enjoying its summer season. Similar features were also seen in 1903, 1960, and 1990.

In November 2007 a hurricane blew up in a region of Saturn's southern hemisphere known to NASA scientists as Storm Alley. Since the orbiting *Cassini* probe could not keep constant watch, the experts relied on the contributions of backyard stargazers to monitor it. The storm, thousands of miles wide, was still raging months later, producing lightning bolts 10,000 times more powerful than those that occur on Earth.

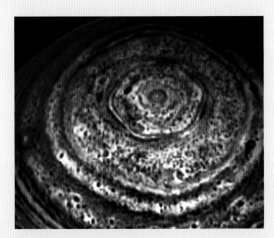

The strange six-sided feature around Saturn's north pole imaged by *Cassini's* visual and infrared mapping spectrometer.

POLAR WIND

Spacecraft have discovered that monster hurricanes are raging at both of Saturn's poles. Winds blow clockwise at 350 miles per hour (560 kmph) in a storm 5,000 miles (8,050 km) wide at the south—two-thirds the diameter of Earth. An even bigger tempest at the north pole, first spotted by the Voyager probes in the 1980s, is nearly 15,000 miles (25,000 km) across and is, curiously, hexagonal in shape.

LIGHTING-UP TIME

Auroras have been observed in Saturn's atmosphere. Recent studies suggest that these, like similar glows on Jupiter, are caused by charged particles raining down from Saturn's magnetic field, which is stronger than Earth's but weaker than Jupiter's. As with Jupiter, these particles seem originally to have been ejected by its moons.

BLOWING HOT AND COLD

In the cold outer reaches of the solar system, Saturn's cloud tops manage a temperature of only -285°F (-175°C). But once you delve deep inside, things start to warm up. Saturn gives off about 2.5 times as much heat as it receives from the Sun, and the temperature at the core soars to a surprising 21,000°F (11,700°C). Scientists believe that as the helium sinks through the liquid hydrogen, gravity separates the two gases and generates an intense heat—a similar process to one occurring in the Sun, albeit on a far smaller scale. Around Saturn's core, as with Jupiter, is found a layer of hydrogen, which is compressed into a metal-like state. This becomes a liquid layer before blending into a gaseous atmosphere.

This picture combines standard views with infrared images. They were taken by the *Cassini* probe from beneath the unlit side of the blue rings while the planet's night side glows red. The part of the planet in sunlight shines in sapphire and mint green.

> *"When I saw the spot, I admit I felt excited. I telephoned Dr. Steavenson at once, just to be sure I was not 'seeing things.'"*

—WILL HAY, MOVIE STAR AND AMATEUR ASTRONOMER

EXCITING TITAN

Dutch astronomer Christiaan Huygens spotted a starlike point remaining close to Saturn in March 1655—he had discovered its first satellite. Later named Titan, it is the only moon besides our own to have been visited by a space probe—the Cassini-Huygens mission, named in honor of the moon's discoverer and his clever contemporary Giovanni Cassini.

The incredible view of Titan's rock-strewn surface that greeted *Huygens* space probe when it landed in January 2005.

Features strongly resembling river channels and deltas were imaged by *Huygens* during its descent through Titan's atmosphere.

An artist imagines the view of the space probe *Huygens* sitting on Titan's surface, its parachute trailing across the terrain.

HIDDEN TREASURE

Titan is Saturn's largest satellite, and, with a diameter of 3,200 miles (5,150 km), it is the second biggest moon in the solar system—also even bigger than Mercury. It is mainly composed of water ice and rock, and its surface is hidden beneath a thick atmosphere denser than Earth's. *Voyager 1*, the first space probe sent to get a close view of Titan, returned somewhat disappointing images in 1980, when it failed to penetrate the orange haze that surrounds the moon. An infrared camera on the Hubble space telescope picked up hints of two features that were named Xanadu and Shangri-la.

The big breakthrough in learning what Titan's surface is really like came only with an ambitious joint mission by NASA and the ESA. As the *Cassini* mothership approached Saturn to go into orbit, it fired a separate probe, *Huygens*, toward the planet's biggest moon. To the delight of mission scientists, *Huygens* made a soft landing on the surface of Titan in January 2005 and sent back a photograph of a rocky landscape. During the three-hour descent, *Huygens* returned a wealth of data to Earth.

THE GREAT LAKES

As *Huygens* parachuted gently through Titan's nitrogen-rich atmosphere, it took images of its surroundings, revealing features that resembled rivers and shorelines. Mission scientists were prepared for the craft to land in an ocean and sink, but in the end it touched down on a spongy surface that resembled a damp, former lake bed. The rocks it pictured were well rounded, indicating that they had been eroded by liquid, like pebbles on a beach.

Huygens's observations have been enhanced by data from *Cassini* as it makes regular close approaches to Titan during its orbit of Saturn. Cloud-piercing radar and other instruments have revealed that Titan resembles Earth in many ways. Surface features have been shaped by wind and rain, and *Cassini* mapped a vast region of lakes and small seas in the North. But, though the weather cycle is like our own, Titan rain is not water but methane or ethane.

A FAMILIAR LANDSCAPE

Hubble's Xanadu was revealed to be a "continent" the size of Australia. Dark sand dunes on its western edge give way to rivers, hills, and valleys. Elsewhere *Cassini* imaged a 93-mile (150-km) range of mountains 1 mile (1.6 km) high, topped with hydrocarbon snow. It was all strangely reminiscent of features back home.

SWIMMING WITH LIFE?

Scientists are excited by Titan because it is so rich in organic compounds. They believe it could be like the brew that nourished life on Earth. The *Cassini* probe also found strong evidence for a huge sea of water and ammonia beneath the surface. Radar mapping showed that features on the ground are moving, and scientists think this means Titan's crust is separated from its core by an underground ocean. Some wonder whether simple life-forms might already have arisen in this heady mix, kick-started by heat from the core.

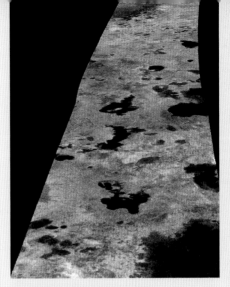

Cassini's cloud-piercing radar has built up pictures of Titan's own lake district, replenished by raining fuel such as methane.

BALLOON MISSION

Planetary scientists are eager to send further missions to Titan, including a balloon to sail through the atmosphere and rovers to crawl on the surface. The planned mission, called Tandem, would also dispatch a probe to another organic-rich moon of Saturn, Enceladus.

An enhanced shot from *Cassini* of Titan's orange globe encircled by a thin halo of purple, light-scattering haze.

MYRIAD MOONS

Saturn's ninth moon, Phoebe—the first photographic discovery—was found in 1899. A tenth, Janus, was not seen until 1966, but dozens more have been found since. It is virtually impossible to distinguish between the smallest of the satellites and the countless "moonlets" that are the largest particles of rock within Saturn's rings.

Heavily cratered Phoebe appears to be an ice-rich body coated with a thin layer of dark material.

MIMAS AND ENCELADUS

Mimas is 260 miles (418 km) wide at most and is the closest and smallest of the big seven moons of Saturn. A heavily cratered, icy world, it bears one scar from an impact that must have almost broken it apart. The Herschel Crater, named after William Herschel, the man who discovered it in 1789, is nearly a third of the moon's diameter and gives Mimas an uncanny resemblance to the Death Star in the *Star Wars* movies.

Herschel also first spotted Enceladus in 1789. It is 318 miles (512 km) across and very different from Mimas. This geologically active moon is crossed by "tiger stripes"—fissures that squirt vast plumes of water ice into space. The *Cassini* probe flew through one of these geysers in March 2008 and found it to contain organic chemicals that could make it another place for us to search for microbial life. Icy particles ejected from Enceladus form one of Saturn's fainter adornments, the E-ring.

Cassini captures a plume of icy particles and water vapor being blasted into space from Enceladus.

TETHYS, DIONE, AND RHEA

Tethys, discovered by astronomer Giovanni Cassini in 1684, is 666 miles (1,072 km) wide and another heavily cratered ice world. It has a vast, shallow crater 250 miles (400 km) wide, called Odysseus, plus an ancient grand canyon called Ithaca Chasma. The moon's highly reflective surface is thought to be the result of particles blasted from Saturn's E-ring, created by Enceladus's icy volcanoes.

A look down toward the south pole of Tethys, showing the giant rift Ithaca Chasma that cuts across the surface.

A beautiful view of Dione against the shadows of the rings on Saturn's cloud tops. The rings themselves can be seen almost edge-on.

Dione, also discovered by Cassini that same year, is a world of rock and ice measuring 696 miles (1,120 km) in diameter. Scientists were surprised to see wispy markings on its surface in distant views from Voyager spacecraft in the early 1980s. Were they floes of volcanic ice? No. Detailed images from *Cassini* a quarter of a century later reveal that the bright pattern is formed of cliffs of ice where the crust has fractured.

Rhea, at 956 miles (1,538 km) wide, is Saturn's second biggest moon and another that was first seen by Cassini in 1672. Few places in the solar system show such heavy scarring, and the craters include two ancient impact basins. The *Cassini* probe photographed wispy markings, which may have been caused by fractures in the surface. A surprise discovery in March 2008 was that Rhea appears to be encircled by faint dusty rings of its own.

IAPETUS

Iapetus, which Cassini spotted in 1671, is 900 miles (1,450 km) wide. It has long intrigued astronomers since it appears far brighter at one stage of its orbit than at others. Cassini suggested that Iapetus always keeps the same face toward Saturn and that one hemisphere must be darker than the other, and space probes have proved him right. Scientists used to believe that the dark material was deposited by a darker-colored moon called Phoebe. However, recent research suggests it is a residue left when ice evaporated into space. Another feature is a mountainous ridge around the equator that makes it look as if it has been crafted in a mold.

SHEPHERD MOONS

Many of Saturn's smaller satellites are known as shepherd moons because their gravitational pull helps shape the patterns and gaps in the planet's rings. Peculiar twists and distortions in Saturn's F-ring were shown in summer 2008 to be caused by the influence of tiny moonlets orbiting within it.

SATURN'S RETINUE

Seven of Saturn's moons—Titan, Tethys, Dione, Rhea, Iapetus, Mimas, and Enceladus—are massive enough to have collapsed into a spherical shape. They were named by John Herschel, son of William Herschel, who discovered two of Saturn's moons and the planet Uranus. The smaller siblings of Saturn's seven biggest moons contain an amazing mix of bodies, 25 of which are at least 6 miles (10 km) across.

The peculiar, spongelike moon Hyperion looks quite unlike any other satellite. Its spectacular craters make it resemble a bath sponge. Its greatest width is just 220 miles (355 km).

SPOT SATURN

These are opposition dates for Saturn, which begins 2009 in Leo but moves steadily through neighboring Virgo to reach Libra in 2014:

2009 March 8
2010 March 22
2011 April 4
2012 April 15
2013 April 28
2014 May 10
2015 May 23

CHAPTER TEN

URANUS
AND NEPTUNE

The Sun's family of planets was once thought to end at Saturn. The five that we have visited so far—plus Earth, of course—are worlds known since the dawn of history, and it apparently did not occur to anyone that there might be other planets yet undiscovered. News that a new planet lurked beyond the ringed giant must therefore have rocked the scientific establishment like an earthquake.

William Herschel's discovery of Uranus in 1781 pushed back the boundaries of the solar system—but there was more to come with the finding of another planet, Neptune, just 65 years later. These were no minor additions to the club. Both are enormous worlds smaller only than Jupiter and Saturn. They are such similar worlds that they have sometimes been considered twins—and if Jupiter and Saturn are gas giants, this pair can be thought of as ice giants. Each has moons of its own and an opaque atmosphere that long left scientists wondering what lay within. Space probes have only paid them passing visits, but these vehicles and improved observing tools used by astronomers are finally unlocking the secrets of these denizens of the deep.

WHAT WE KNEW THEN

Earthbound astronomers could make out no surface details. By weighing the worlds, however, they determined that these planets were far less dense than Earth, and so they might resemble Jupiter and Saturn and be covered by clouds.

WHAT WE THINK WE KNOW NOW

Uranus and Neptune are both denser than the gas giants, Jupiter and Saturn. Beneath the clouds both planets are believed to be packed with a soupy mix of much more of the ice and rock that their bigger cousins only have at their cores.

The peculiar tipped-up moon Triton hangs above Neptune, bright clouds and dark spots visible in the planet's bluish atmosphere.

"Then felt I like some watcher of the skies
When a new planet swims into his ken."

—JOHN KEATS

URANUS: BRAVE NEW WORLD

The discovery of Uranus was made by a military deserter who went on to become one of the greatest figures in astronomy—William Herschel. It brought him worldwide fame and the attention of royalty, but he was very lucky that the new world had not been recognized as such before, because it had been spotted many times.

William Herschel holds a sketch of his newly discovered planet Uranus in this portrait by John Russell.

HOOKED ON THE HEAVENS

Herschel was born in Hanover, Germany, in 1738 to a musical family. He signed up for the band of the Hanoverian Guard, but after an unpleasant skirmish with French invaders, fled to England. He became an organist at Bath, giving music lessons to boost his meager income. Herschel decided he wanted a telescope and, when he found he could not easily buy one, decided to make one himself. Herschel's first views through his new instrument hooked him on the heavens; he forgot about music as he followed his new calling. Herschel lived and made his telescopes at a modest row house at 19 New King Street, Bath, observing the sky from his small backyard—light pollution was clearly less of a problem in towns and cities in the eighteenth century.

A DIM DOT

Despite going unrecognized before Herschel, Uranus is actually just bright enough to be seen with the naked eye on a clear, dark night away from streetlights. It is easy to see with binoculars, though it will still resemble a star; however, a telescope will reveal the tiny blue-green disk.

A STAR LIKE NO OTHER

On March 13, 1781, Herschel was looking at stars above a certain brightness when he chanced upon one that showed as a tiny disk instead of a starlike point of light. Herschel continued to observe the object over the following few nights and confirmed that it moved against the starry backdrop. Despite its disklike appearance, however, Herschel believed that he had found a comet rather than a new planet.

England's Astronomer Royal of the day, Nevil Maskelyne, suspected that the new object was really a planet, and this was confirmed by follow-up observations that allowed its orbit to be plotted, indicating it to be twice as far from Earth as Saturn. In a blatant act of toadying, Herschel named the planet Georgium Sidus, Latin for "George's Star," as a tribute to King George III. Predictably, this did not go down very well with England's long-term rivals, the French, who chose to call it Herschel instead. Both of these breaks with the naming tradition were rejected by the astronomical authorities, however. Instead they chose to give the planet the name of the Greek god of the sky—Uranus.

FAME AND FORTUNE

Herschel's discovery was an accident, but as he himself pointed out, it did not happen by chance. He was methodically examining constellations star by star, and as he later said, "it was that night its turn to be discovered." The very first discovery of a planet brought Herschel great fame. The king of England, George III, summoned him to Windsor to show the royal family the stars and created a new position for him of King's Astronomer—the post of Astronomer Royal being already taken—with a salary of £200 a year. Herschel's achievements also earned him a royal pardon for his military desertion, which was presented to him by the king.

EARLY VIEWS

In fact, Uranus had not gone totally unnoticed before Herschel's discovery. England's first Astronomer Royal, John Flamsteed, made several sightings of it from 1690 onward but mistook it every time for a star. And a rare eighteenth-century star atlas by John Bevis, the *Atlas Celeste*, shows a nonexistent star in Sagittarius precisely where Uranus would have been located in the summer of 1738. Uranus also crops up in the prediscovery records of other observers.

"William Herschel was possibly the greatest observer who ever lived."

—Sir Patrick Moore, British astronomer, TV personality, and author

The fame and fortune that finding Uranus brought Herschel allowed him to build this giant 40-foot (12.2-m) telescope with a 48-inch (122-cm) mirror at Slough, England.

A replica of the telescope with which Herschel discovered Uranus is kept at his house, now a museum, in Bath, England.

William Herschel was a member of the Lunar Society, a regular gathering in Birmingham of the greatest minds of his day.

URANUS: SIDLING ALONG

When astronomers watched the first known moons of Uranus orbit the planet, it became clear that there was something very strange about this remote world, which takes more than 84 years to orbit the Sun. The planet is, in effect, lying on its side.

This look back at Uranus as *Voyager 2* sped past in January 1986 is a crescent view that would be impossible to see from Earth.

SPOT URANUS

Uranus crawls from Aquarius in 2009 into Pisces where it lurks for the next 10 years.

A TIPPED-UP WORLD

Unlike the satellites of other planets, the moons of Uranus were found to be orbiting at a remarkably steep angle. This gave astronomers a clue to one of the most remarkable characteristics of the seventh planet—its axis is tilted by nearly 98 degrees to the plane of the ecliptic. The calamity that caused this can only be imagined, but it was most likely caused by a cosmic hit-and-run by another body billions of years ago.

Uranus's tilt means that it must experience extraordinary seasons, even though it lies too far away to receive much heat from the Sun. One hemisphere will spend many years in sunlight before being slowly turned away to face years of darkness while the other hemisphere basks in the light. Equinoxes, which happen every six months on Earth, occur 42 years apart on Uranus. The most recent time this occurred was December 2007, when Uranus's north pole saw the Sun for the first time in more than four decades.

STORMY WEATHER

Some of the fastest winds in the solar system have been detected on Uranus, blowing at more than 500 miles per hour (800 kmph). Storms, which show as bright spots in infrared pictures, tend to line up at particular latitudes.

The Kuiper Airborne Observatory first detected the existence of several rings around Uranus as it watched a star blink on and off.

THE PLANET'S STAR TURN

Until 1977, Saturn was considered unique in the solar system for its fine system of rings. But that year it lost this distinction when rings were found to encircle Uranus, too. It was a discovery made entirely by chance. The planet was due to perform an extremely rare occultation by passing in front of a background star as seen from Earth. Scientists using a flying telescope, NASA's Kuiper Airborne Observatory, were eager to study the event on March 10, 1977, to try to learn more about Uranus's atmosphere. What they did not expect was to see the star suddenly blink five times before and five times after it went behind the planet. Although they were not directly visible, it was clear that there must be a ring system there. The space probe *Voyager 2* viewed the rings, and they have also been photographed by the Hubble space telescope. The number of known distinct rings has increased to 13. They are thought to be relatively young and the remains of a shattered moon.

TEASING OUT THE DETAIL

Though astronomers were able to make out a disk for Herschel's new planet, it was frustratingly devoid of even the slightest detail, so they had no idea what it really looked like or how fast it rotated. Even when *Voyager 2* flew past in 1985, the planet refused to give up its secrets. Images showed just a bluish green disk with none of the patterns that decorate the clouds of Jupiter and Saturn. Finally, the Hubble space telescope broke through the barrier in the 1990s, peering deep into Uranus's atmosphere with the aid of infrared filters. It revealed clear and hazy layers as well as many occasional bright clouds. False color was used to highlight different layers, and the dark rings were artificially brightened to show them more clearly.

Uranus's atmosphere is made up mainly of hydrogen and helium, plus methane, which accounts for the bluish color. Deep down there are clouds of water and ammonia ice, and possibly an ocean of liquid water. Temperatures may reach up to 12,600°F (7,000°C) in its rocky core but manage only around −355°F (−215°C) in the atmosphere.

LIVING ON THE EDGE

Because Uranus reached one of its equinoxes in 2007, there have been times recently when its ring system was turned edge-on to Earth. The Hubble space telescope was able to capture one of these rare occasions in August 2007; the rings looked like spikes sticking out above and below the planet. This was the first time they had ever been seen in this way because, on previous occasions when they were tilted in this manner, no one had known the rings existed.

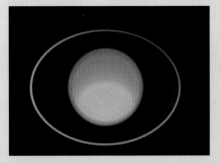

A photograph taken in infrared light by the Hubble space telescope in 1995 picks out the rings and different layers in Uranus's atmosphere.

Another enhanced image from Hubble in 1998 shows Uranus surrounded by four major rings, several moons, and clouds above the planet.

URANUS'S SATELLITES

URANUS'S SAT

SATELLITE ORBITS OF URANUS

An illustration of Uranus and the orbits of its five larger satellites, Miranda, Ariel, Umbriel, Titania, and Oberon.

William Herschel discovered the first two of Uranus's 27 known satellites in 1787. Two more were found by British brewing tycoon William Lassell in 1851, and a fifth, Miranda, by U.S. astronomer Gerard Kuiper in 1948. The moons of Uranus are all named after characters from either the works of Shakespeare or another English poet, Alexander Pope.

ENTER STAGE RIGHT

Voyager 2 detected 10 smaller satellites as it flew past Uranus: Juliet, Puck, Cordelia, Ophelia, Bianca, Desdemona, Portia, Rosalind, Cressida, and Belinda. An 11th was later found in the images from the probe. These are inner moons and are all made of rock and ice. Eleven smaller moons have since been spotted. These are tiny, sometimes only 10 miles (16 km) or less wide; they are thought to be captured asteroids.

CRASH COURSE

Shepherd moons Cordelia and Ophelia control the shape of the outer ring of Uranus. Eight small satellites orbit between these moons and Miranda in a region so crowded that they threaten to crash into one another.

DRAMATIS PERSONAE

Miranda, which has a diameter of 290 miles (470 km), is the closest of the main moons to Uranus and the most active geologically. Tidal forces are believed to have helped to create a chaotic, cratered landscape like our own lunar highlands but with vast canyons, fractures, and features caused by eruptions of icy lava. Three strange oval features resemble crazy racetracks.

Ariel, with a diameter measuring 720 miles (1,158 km), is one of Herschel's original discoveries. Our only close-up view came from *Voyager 2*, which revealed an icy, pockmarked world crossed by countless valleys and faults, filled with frosty deposits.

Umbriel is the black sheep of the family, being much less bright than its major siblings. It has a diameter of 726 miles (1,169 km) and

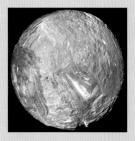

Miranda's crazy landscape, which includes canyons, cracks, lava flows, and strange "racetracks" is shaped by tidal forces.

Voyager 2's most detailed view of Ariel revealed valleys, scarps, and extensive cratering. Icy deposits fill many of the grooves.

appears to be relatively inactive geologically, with an ancient, heavily cratered surface. From the limited view that was obtained by *Voyager 2*, one curious bright ring near the equator stands out. Named Wunda, it is not known whether it is a volcanic crater or caused by a recent impact.

"ILL MET BY MOONLIGHT..."

Titania, at 1,000 miles (1,600 km) wide, is the largest of Uranus's moons, and the eighth biggest satellite in the solar system. It comprises a mixture of rock, ice, and organic compounds. Its cratered moonscape includes a rift that would dwarf our own Grand Canyon and a huge basin—185 miles (300 km) wide— named Gertrude.

Oberon is the most distant of Uranus's five big moons and, with a diameter measuring 945 miles (1,520 km), the second largest. Once again we only have the images from *Voyager 2* to show us what Oberon's surface is like, but the ancient craters of this icy world indicate signs of more recent geological activity. Oberon also boasts a mountain many miles high that looks like a pimple poking above the moon's limb.

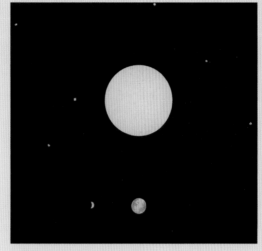

A sketch of Uranus, complete with moons and background stars, from 1849 when some still called the planet Herschel.

THE RIDDLE OF THE RING

William Herschel claimed to have suspected that he saw a reddish ring around Uranus in 1789, nearly two centuries before they were confirmed. Because the rings are so dark and no other observers reported anything similar, it is generally assumed that Herschel must have imagined them.

Umbriel's dark, ancient, cratered surface is decorated with a few mysterious, bright icy rings.

As well as impact scarring, Titania shows evidence that it has undergone geological activity, such as movements in its crust.

Oberon has an icy, cratered, terrain that includes a mountain pimple seen peeking over the limb at lower left from *Voyager 2*.

NEPTUNE: EIGHTH WONDER

With one new planet already found, it was not long before astronomers were given indications that yet another world lurked deep in the solar system. Eighth planet Neptune was located not simply by scanning the heavens but, for the first time, by the application of human computing power.

John Couch Adams, pictured as a young man, carried out calculations in England to pinpoint the position of an eighth planet in the solar system.

PULLING POWER

A tracking of Uranus's long journey around the Sun showed that it did not always appear exactly where it might be expected if the influence of only the known planets was taken into account. It was clear that there could be another body, as yet unknown, exerting a pull on the seventh planet. Unknown to each other, two mathematicians—John Couch Adams in England and Urbain Le Verrier in France—set out independently to try to calculate where in space this new world must lie.

HUNT THE PLANET

Adams reached a conclusion in 1845 and urged the Astronomer Royal, Sir George Airy, to instigate a search in the area he had divined. Airy prevaricated, asking for more information, and after Adams failed to reply, the search did not go ahead. It also cannot have helped that British astronomers did not have particularly detailed star charts. Meanwhile, in Paris, Le Verrier was tackling the same problem and published a paper revealing where he thought the new planet must lie. Airy saw the paper and realized that Le Verrier's result put the undiscovered planet very close to that calculated by Adams. At last, in July 1846, Airy instigated a search by Professor James Challis of Cambridge Observatory. Challis scoured the sky throughout August and September.

Unfortunately for the British, Le Verrier had called on astronomers at Berlin Observatory, who had recently equipped themselves with superior star charts. Johann Galle received Le Verrier's letter on September 23, 1846, and

Urbain Le Verrier discusses the discovery of Neptune with the French king, Louis-Philippe, in Paris.

Johann Galle was the man who first knowingly set eyes on the eighth planet on the very day he started searching.

Voyager 2 took this snapshot of Neptune, including a dark spot and bright clouds, in 1989 from a distance of 4.4 million miles (7.08 million km).

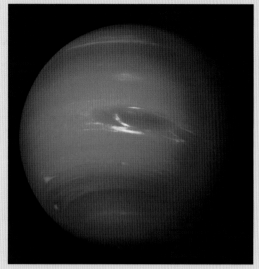

A SECOND FIND

Just 17 days after the discovery of Neptune, the wealthy English amateur astronomer William Lassell spotted a moon orbiting around it, which was named Triton. It remained Neptune's only known companion for 103 years.

spotted the new planet the very same night, close to Saturn and little more than a moon's breadth from the predicted position in Aquarius.

MISSED OPPORTUNITIES

Challis was mortified to find that he had logged the new planet twice in the early days of his search, on August 8 and 12. But he claimed he had been too busy processing old comet observations to notice. In fact, Neptune had been spotted as far back as 1612 by none other than Galileo, who noted it very close to Jupiter in December that year and in January 1613 but simply logged it as a star.

Galileo was not the only one to miss out. French astronomer Jérôme Lalande observed Neptune twice, on May 8 and 12, 1795, while compiling a star catalog, the *Histoire Céleste*. Sadly, he discarded his first observation, presuming he had made a mistake, and only included the second.

A CROSS-CHANNEL SCRAP

With centuries of bitter rivalry already behind them, the almost simultaneous discoveries of Neptune sparked fierce new controversy between England and France. The French were aghast when John Herschel proposed that Adams should share the glory because he had communicated his results to the Astronomer Royal. However, Adams was magnanimous in acknowledging the prior claim of Le Verrier.

ALL AT SEA

Le Verrier initially put forward the classical name Neptune, after the Roman god of the sea, for his new world, against rival suggestions of Janus from Galle and Oceanus from Challis. Although Le Verrier apparently changed his mind and wanted to name the planet after himself, the astronomical authorities swiftly adopted his earlier suggestion.

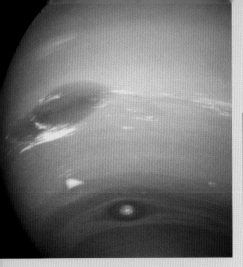

Weather features on Neptune, including the dark spot, were captured by *Voyager 2* during its flyby in 1989.

"Neptune is an efficient weather machine compared to Earth. It seems to run on almost no energy."

—LAWRENCE A. SROMOVSKY,
UNIVERSITY OF
WISCONSIN–MADISON

NEPTUNE'S WORLD

Neptune takes nearly 165 years to orbit the Sun, which means that it has barely completed one circuit since it was discovered. At nearly 2.8 billion miles (4.5 billion km) from the Sun, Neptune is more than half as far away again as Uranus and only a seventh as bright.

BLOWING IN THE WIND

Neptune is slightly smaller than Uranus but very similar in nature. It is even bluer, if anything, because it has more methane in its atmosphere along with hydrogen, ammonia, and water. The visible surface is by no means bland. *Voyager 2* flew past in 1989, revealing some deep blue bands and a huge dark storm half the size of Jupiter's Great Red Spot, which was, inevitably, instantly nicknamed the Great Dark Spot. Hubble observations suggest it has since vanished, however. *Voyager 2* also spotted bright clouds zipping along at incredible speeds of up to 700 miles per hour (1,100 kmph). Beneath the clouds, increasingly dense gases are thought to become a liquid layer around Neptune's rocky core.

THE VOICE OF SEASON

Neptune's axis is tilted by 28 degrees, a few more than Earth's, meaning that it also experiences seasons during its 165-year trip around the Sun, though not as extreme as those of Uranus.

YET MORE RINGS

Voyager 2 confirmed that Neptune also has rings—their existence had been suspected ever since astronomers saw stars blinking behind them. There are six barely visible, dusty, twisted rings—though they are more like arcs, being much denser in some parts than others. They are thought to be young and not expected to last long. William Lassell thought he saw a ring soon after the planet was discovered, but this was caused by a defect in his telescope.

An image from *Voyager 2* is enhanced to show the two brightest rings of the six that are known to encircle Neptune.

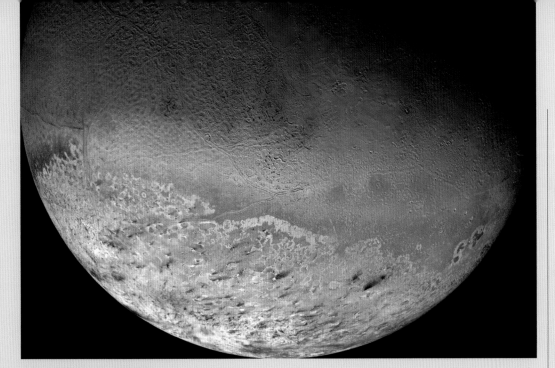

Voyager's **close-up** view of Triton shows that it is mottled like a melon, with huge cracks and erupting geysers.

SPOT NEPTUNE

In 2009 and 2010, Neptune is due to wander between Capricornus and Aquarius, which you can find on your planisphere (*see page 148*). It will not be visible with the naked eye, but it may be spotted with binoculars at magnitude 8.

TANTALIZING TRITON

Neptune has fewer satellites than the other giant planets, and most of the 13 known are a mixture of small rocks of little substance. The exception is Triton, which is a respectable 1,680 miles (2,705 km) in diameter and spherical. It is also unique in the solar system as the only major moon that orbits backward—its axis is tilted by 157 degrees to that of Neptune.

Voyager 2 captured a really good view of the moon as it flew past in 1989, and this revealed a strikingly mottled terrain like a cantaloupe (muskmelon), crossed by a few ridges and valleys. A lack of craters plus the sight of several spouting geysers showed that this is an active world. Above a surface coating of pink frost lies a thin atmosphere of nitrogen and methane. Triton is also much denser and rockier than most moons of the outer planets. This, along

with its strange orbit, has led astronomers to conclude that the satellite is really an object that Neptune captured from an outer region called the Kuiper Belt when it ventured too close. Since the slightly smaller Pluto is now also thought to be from the Kuiper Belt, it follows that *Voyager*'s view of Triton could be telling us what Pluto really looks like.

ECCENTRIC NEREID

The second of Neptune's moons to be found— by U.S. astronomer Gerard Kuiper in 1949— was Nereid. *Voyager 2* revealed that Nereid has an irregular shape and is about 210 miles (340 km) across. It is most notable for having the most eccentric orbits known for a satellite, its distance from Neptune ranging from just 841,100 miles (1.35 million km) to 5.98 million miles (9.62 million km).

An artist's impression of Neptune, complete with rings, as seen from the moon Nereid.

CHAPTER ELEVEN

PLUTO AND BEYOND

And so we come to poor Pluto, our "lost" planet. The god of the underworld became the underdog of the solar system when, in 2006, astronomy's arbiters, the IAU, redefined what makes a planet a planet. Pluto's failure to make the grade was particularly felt in the United States, which found itself losing the only planet to have been discovered from its shores. The IAU may not have foreseen the wave of protest, much of it sentimental, as some argued that cultural perceptions and history need to be taken into account as much as scientific reasoning. But astronomers had to do something.

In recent years a wave of discoveries had shown that Pluto is not alone in the remoter regions of the solar system, but is a prominent member in a swarm of perhaps millions of icy objects. The largest of these, including Pluto, are now dwarf planets that have been newly termed plutoids.

Pluto itself has not changed. It is still there, following its long path around the sun and as fascinating as ever. Indeed, it might have become even more intriguing, standing as it does at the gateway to a new realm, the recognition of which proves that our understanding of the solar system is forever changing.

"Excited? I should say so!"

—Clyde Tombaugh, discoverer of Pluto

WHAT WE KNEW THEN

The discovery of Pluto in 1930 was hailed as the most important astronomical event in nearly 100 years. Initial reports wrongly suggested it was bigger than Earth. Interestingly, the telegram announcing the discovery hesitated to claim a new planet, terming it "a trans-Neptunian body." Some astronomers wondered if it might be an escaped moon of Neptune.

WHAT WE THINK WE KNOW NOW

The IAU introduced three main rules that a body had to meet to be called a planet:
1. It must orbit the Sun;
2. It must be big and heavy enough to have collapsed into a spherical shape under the force of its own gravity; and
3. It must have cleared the area around its orbital path.

Deep in the solar system, Pluto, accompanied by its larger moon Charon and smaller attendants Nix and Hydra, glides in front of a distant Sun.

THE SEARCH IS ON

After the discovery of Neptune, some astronomers believed that another undiscovered world must still be exerting influence on Uranus, and they set out to find it. Among them was Percival Lowell, who built an observatory at Flagstaff, Arizona, to help him study the canals that he was convinced covered Mars.

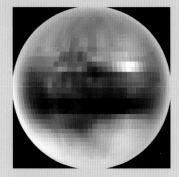

This crude map of Pluto was constructed by measuring subtle brightness variations as the world was eclipsed by its largest moon, Charon.

X MARKS THE SPOT

The search for Lowell's Planet X began in 1905, but nothing had been found by the time of his death in 1916, despite Pluto being captured in photos twice without anyone realizing it in March 1915. The Lowell Observatory's search did not resume until 1929, when self-taught astronomer Clyde Tombaugh from Kansas joined the staff. He was put to work photographing the sky and poring over the images of millions of stars. Nearly a year after he had begun his work, on February 18, 1930, Tombaugh spotted a candidate for Planet X while examining images of Gemini taken the previous month. Additional photos confirmed the discovery, and it was announced to the world on March 13, 1930.

BLINK AND YOU'LL FIND IT

Searching through so many stars sounds like an impossible task, but Tombaugh's job was eased by a device called a blink comparator, which superimposed pairs of images taken on different nights and flipped between them. Any object that had appeared or moved would become obvious as it blinked on and off.

I NAME THIS WORLD

Pluto was discovered in the same year that Walt Disney created the cartoon pooch who shares that name. But, contrary to the belief of some, that is not how the distant world acquired its moniker—for that we have to thank an 11-year-old English girl, Venetia Burney. Her grandfather, Falconer Madan, told her about the new discovery as he read his newspaper at the breakfast table on March 14, 1930. He added that it had not yet been named.

Venetia, who was interested in mythology and astronomy, suggested the name of Pluto after the Roman god of the underworld. Her grandfather was so impressed with this idea that he went to tell his friend, an astronomy professor at the University of Oxford, Herbert Hall Turner. When the professor heard Venetia's suggestion he sent a telegram to the Lowell Observatory, whose staff unanimously picked the name from a short list of three. Six weeks later the name Pluto was announced officially, and Mr. Madan rewarded his granddaughter with a prize of £5.

Clyde Tombaugh is pictured at the door of the Lowell Observatory, where he discovered Pluto in 1930.

INCREDIBLE SHRINKING WORLD

With Pluto too far away to show a disk, astronomers had to guess its size. Assuming it was affecting the orbits of Uranus and Neptune, they first estimated a mass similar to Earth's, but when studies conducted in 1976 showed that the surface must be methane ice, they realized it had to be less than a hundredth the estimated size to display the brightness it does. When Pluto's biggest moon, Charon, was found in 1978, astronomers were able to apply the laws formulated by Kepler and Newton to derive a diameter of 1,400 miles (2,300 km). Pluto is not visible in small backyard telescopes because it only reaches magnitude 14.

DISK DETAIL

By employing advanced optical techniques, astronomers have just managed to discern the disk of Pluto. The closest we have gotten to any detail is in images taken by the Hubble space telescope. These have mapped about 12 bright and dark areas. The bright areas are thought to be frozen nitrogen, while the dark may be methane frost.

THE X FILES

Pluto turned out to be far too small to have a significant influence on other planets' orbits, so it could not be the fabled Planet X. Astronomers subsequently found that the disturbances to Uranus's path were caused by an incorrect judgment of Neptune's mass.

JUNE, 1930   POPULAR SCIENCE MONTHLY   27

How They Trailed a New Planet

Study of many photos of stars disclosed to a farm boy what may prove a new world where a famous astronomer said it would be. Old theories are upset by find.

By
ALDEN P. ARMAGNAC

A NEW planet has been announced. Out in space, four billion miles beyond the globe we live on, a yellowish object, a little larger than the earth, swings in a vast circle about the sun; a frigid little world, bathed in the dim light of perpetual dusk. Its discovery is called the most important event in astronomy in nearly a hundred years.

A new planet is not found every day. As many of us learned in school, a planet is one of the exclusive company of heavenly bodies that get their light and heat from the sun. They swing about it, as the earth does, in great circular paths, or orbits. These earthlike worlds are so few in number that they may be counted on the fingers.

Six, visible to the naked eye, were known to the ancients. In outward order from the sun they are: Mercury, Venus, Earth, Mars, Jupiter, and Saturn. Only two more, far-away Uranus and Neptune, were added comparatively recently when peering at the sky with telescopes came into fashion.

Now there is a ninth.
The ninth awaits positive confirmation.

It behaves differently from other planets. Its orbit is so far from a perfect circle, and tilted so askew, that astronomers hesitate to declare it a planet with certainty. Yet its actions are even less like any known comet, or anything else that might be mistaken for a planet.

There is one compelling reason to believe the newcomer is really the ninth planet. Astronomers of the Lowell Observatory, at Flagstaff, Ariz., found it remarkably near the spot where the late Doctor Perci-

On the outer rim of the solar system whirls the new planet. This perspective view shows the planets in about the positions they occupied when the ninth member of the family was first sighted by man.

Above, the starry waste with its planets and suns as seen through a powerful telescope. It was in a maze of this sort, with its myriad pin points of light, that the new faintly glowing planet, hardly visible, was found.

A contemporary report of the discovery of Pluto reveals that even in 1930 there was some doubt over its status as a planet.

FROM HERO TO ZERO

There were signs early on that Pluto was not like the other planets. First of all, its orbit around the sun is tipped at a steep angle of 17 degrees to the ecliptic. Secondly, that orbit is highly eccentric, ranging from 2.75 billion miles (4.4 billion km) when closest to the Sun to 4.6 billion miles (7.4 billion km) when most distant.

Pluto is the brightest object in this photo taken with the Hubble space telescope with, from left, its moons Charon, Nix, and Hydra.

WE'VE BEEN HERE BEFORE

The debate over Pluto's status is not unprecedented. The first asteroids to be discovered back in the early nineteenth century—including Ceres, Pallas, and Juno—were happily considered planets until astronomers began collecting too many of them. They were swiftly demoted to the new category of asteroid.

An artist imagines the scene as the probe *New Horizons* flies past Pluto, with its main moon Charon visible in the distance.

INCLINED TO STRAY

Pluto's eccentric orbit can bring it closer to the sun than Neptune, and it last came within Neptune's orbit between January 21, 1979, and February 11, 1999. Its inclination means that it can stray far from the ecliptic, too.

PLUTO'S PARTNERS

Pluto was discovered to have a moon in 1978 by astronomers at an outpost of the U.S. Naval Observatory—fittingly at Flagstaff, Arizona, where Pluto had been found. They called it Charon after the ferryman who carried the souls of the dead across the River Styx to the underworld, where the god Pluto was king. Its diameter was estimated at 750 miles (1,210 km), more than half that of Pluto. The two worlds are both tidally locked, keeping the same face toward each other, making this a very unusual pairing. But there were still more discoveries. In 2005 two tiny moons with diameters of less than 100 miles (160 km) were spotted on photos taken by the Hubble space telescope. They have been named Hydra and Nix.

PLUTONS AND PLUTOIDS

There was some confusion generated before the decree that changed Pluto's status. First word from that crucial meeting of the IAU was that the number of planets would increase from 9 to 12, with some of the larger minor worlds joining the premier league. The actual vote changed all that, relegating Pluto to a separate class that included planet in its name but shut it out in the cold as a "dwarf planet." The IAU suggested "plutons" as a new name for worlds such as Pluto, which stirred up yet more trouble since the term was already in use by geologists for a type of rock formation. The IAU went back to the drawing board and took another two years to suggest "plutoids" as a replacement in summer 2008. The hope was that this would give Pluto back some of its esteem and placate some of the protestors. Plutoids, like planets, are roughly spherical, but the crucial difference is that they have not swept their regions of space free of other debris.

HORIZONS NEW

The first space probe ever to visit Pluto was already on its way when astronomers changed the status of the distant world. *New Horizons*, launched in January 2006, is the fastest craft ever sent into space, but still will not reach its target until 2015. That Pluto is no longer a planet does not affect the value of the mission, though its principal scientist, Alan Stern, has been one of the fiercest critics of the reclassification.

New Horizons is carrying a small amount of the ashes of the plutoid's discoverer, Clyde Tombaugh—who died in 1997 at the age of 90—in a tiny canister. The probe will speed past Pluto on July 14, 2015, and then on through the Kuiper Belt over the following years. Eventually it will leave our solar system altogether, carrying Tombaugh's remains toward the stars.

NEW LAW OF PHYSICS

New Mexico, former home of Clyde Tombaugh, rushed through a new law declaring Pluto a planet in the wake of the IAU's decision, despite the fact that the outer reaches of the solar system are not generally considered to come under that state's jurisdiction.

NASA's *New Horizons* **probe** blasts off from Cape Canaveral, Florida, in January 2006 on its nine-year journey to distant Pluto.

OUT IN THE COLD

The writing was on the wall for Pluto when astronomers began discovering similar icy bodies in the far reaches of the solar system. Since the first such body was detected in 1992, about a thousand of these icy wanderers have been found, sometimes as pairs orbiting one another, though the true number may run into millions.

THE EYE OF THE SWARM

The zone of icy worlds in the region of Pluto is known as the Kuiper Belt, after Gerard Kuiper, who was one of those who proposed the theoretical existence of something like it. Its known population of Kuiper Belt Objects (KBOs) is growing all the time. Many so-called short-period comets are believed to have come originally from the Kuiper Belt.

KUIPER BELT OBJECTS

1992 QB1: A major find was made in 1992 when a world outside Neptune's orbit was picked up by a U.S. search team. They wanted to call it Smiley, but it remains labeled 1992 QB1—a catalog number that spawned the name cubewano (Q-B-1-OH) for a particular type of object in the Kuiper Belt.

ERIS: A plutoid—found in 2003 by U.S. planet hunter Mike Brown—that appears to be slightly bigger than Pluto but about three times farther away. Originally cataloged as 2003 UB313, it was mischievously given the pseudoclassical nickname Xena, after TV's popular series *Xena: Warrior Princess*, before being officially named Eris in 2006. In 2005 a satellite was spotted orbiting Eris, and it briefly enjoyed the nickname of Gabrielle, another character in the show, before being officially dubbed Dysnomia.

HAUMEA: This plutoid, a third the size of Pluto, was independently discovered by Spanish astronomers and Mike Brown's team. First labeled 2003 EL61, it was nicknamed Santa before the IAU officially named it after the Hawaiian goddess of childbirth and fertility. It has two tiny moons, now named Hi'iaka and Namaka after Haumea's children.

An artist imagines how Quaoar, named after the god of a Native American tribe, might look in the depths of the solar system.

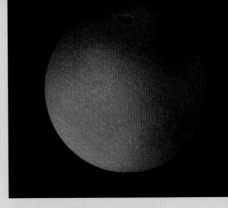

ORCUS: Named after a Roman god of the underworld, Orcus—formerly 2004 KW—is a large KBO in the vicinity of Pluto. It has a 247-year orbit tilted steeply to the ecliptic.

MAKEMAKE: One of the largest of the known KBOs, again found by Brown's team, was first labeled 2005 FY9 and nicknamed Easterbunny. It was later given the name of Makemake—after a traditional deity of the people of Easter Island—and it was designated a plutoid.

QUAOAR: Pronounced "kwa-whar," this is the most distant object in the solar system to be discerned by the Hubble space telescope, after its discovery by Mike Brown and his colleague Chad Trujillo in 2002. Originally labeled 2002 LM60, Quaoar lies about 4 billion miles from Earth and is named after a mythical god of the Tongva tribe from the Los Angeles area. It takes 288 years to orbit the Sun.

VARUNA: First cataloged as 2000 WR106, Varuna was discovered in 2000 by an asteroid-hunting camera on Kitt Peak in Arizona, part of a project called Spacewatch. It is named after the Hindu god of the underworld, and it takes 283 years to orbit the Sun.

THE EDGE OF
THE SOLAR SYSTEM

Beyond the Kuiper Belt, and with much more eccentric and tilted orbits, come a number of icy bodies termed Scattered Disk Objects. More than a thousand times farther out than the Kuiper Belt—and stretching perhaps halfway to the nearest star—is believed to lie what is termed the Oort Cloud. This spherical cloud of icy fragments has never been directly observed,

but it is thought to be the source of the great comets that have visited us throughout history. Astronomers use a general term for bodies in all three zones—Trans-Neptunian Objects.

THE RIDDLE OF SEDNA

One of the most remarkable of these new icy worlds is the Scattered Disk Object Sedna, named after an Inuit goddess. It makes other icy bodies seem positively swift, since it takes more than 12,000 years to orbit the sun. Its extreme orbit means it never comes closer than 7 billion miles (11.5 billion km) and recedes to an incredible 90 billion miles (145 billion km).

STOP THE PRESSES

In August 2008 astronomers announced the discovery of a body like Sedna, but with an even more extended, 22,500-year orbit. Spotted within Neptune's orbit, 2006 SQ372 will travel out to a distance of 150 billion miles—nearly 1,600 times the distance of Earth from the Sun.

An imagined view of Makemake, the plutoid informally known as Easterbunny, and now named after a god from Easter Island.

"'Tis not too late to seek a newer world."

—ALFRED, LORD
TENNYSON

The farthest known world to orbit the Sun is Sedna, whose motion against the stars was first identified in these photos taken in November 2003.

CHAPTER TWELVE

ASTEROIDS AND METEORITES

In the great divide between Mars and Jupiter lies a region that astronomers used to believe was empty space. Right at the start of the nineteenth century, however, observers learned that this was far from the truth. They detected the first of what became a cascade of discoveries of a new type of inhabitant of the solar system—the asteroids. These relatively tiny lumps of rock were considered "space vermin" by some, but they are important to astronomers because they represent some of the oldest objects in the solar system, the building blocks that, in other regions, clumped together to make the planets.

Although most of the millions of asteroids orbit the Sun beyond Mars, a significant number have orbits that bring them close to Earth. Therefore another imperative has developed to find out more about asteroids, and to watch out for any that could one day strike our planet, which would cause untold devastation.

"Between Jupiter and Mars
I place a planet."

—JOHANNES KEPLER

WHAT WE KNEW THEN

As the number of asteroid discoveries began to mount, astronomers thought they were probably viewing the remains of a lost planet that had somehow been smashed to smithereens. Perhaps it had ventured too close to Jupiter, they imagined, or it had been struck by another body passing through the solar system.

WHAT WE THINK WE KNOW NOW

Jupiter is still blamed for the absence of a large planet in the asteroid belt. But, rather than causing one to break up, its gravitational influence prevented these rocks from ever forming a world. Ceres, the largest asteroid, has a rounded form and has recently been reclassified in the new category of dwarf planet.

Asteroids, leftover building blocks of the solar system, tumble through space in the vast gap between Mars and Jupiter.

HUNTING FOR THE LOST PLANET

Astronomers in the eighteenth century became convinced that an undiscovered planet must lie between Mars and Jupiter. Kepler had predicted it, and the gap between the two planets seemed too great otherwise. This began the celestial equivalent of a manhunt.

The Hubble space telescope recorded these pixilated shots of Ceres in 2004 revealing a bright spot as it completed a quarter of a rotation.

A portrait of Giuseppe Piazzi who discovered the first asteroid, Ceres. Like Pluto, it was considered a planet for many years.

CELESTIAL POLICE I

A Hungarian nobleman, Baron Franz von Zach, organized a posse of observers in 1800, and they became known as the Celestial Police. By dividing the sky into a number of individual areas to scour, the officers were each given their own "beat." It was not long before a new world was discovered—though unfortunately for these cosmic cops, it was not made by one of their own but by an independent observer.

THE CELESTIAL POLICE 2

Today's celestial police could be said to be science's official regulators, the International Astronomical Union, or IAU. In 2006, as part of their overhaul of the solar system, they produced new definitions for the types of worlds it contained. At the same time as Pluto was demoted to the new dwarf-planet category, Ceres was promoted to the same class because, with a diameter of 590 miles (950 km), it was massive enough to have formed a roughly spherical shape. The largest of the ordinary asteroids are now Pallas and Vesta, both about 354 miles (570 km) wide at most.

NEW YEAR, NEW WORLD

Giuseppe Piazzi, a Sicilian monk, was checking the sky at Palermo Observatory on New Year's Eve, 1800, when he spotted an unrecorded "star" in the zodiacal constellation of Taurus. He watched it move over the next few weeks, noting that it stayed sharp and starlike, unlike a comet. However, it was lost in twilight before Piazzi announced it and not found again until the following December. Piazzi wanted to call it Ceres Ferdinandea, after the Roman goddess of Sicily and the island's then-ruler, King Ferdinand III, but only the classical name stuck.

Our first close view of an asteroid came in 1991 when the *Galileo* probe visited Gaspra.

The Dawn mission enters the asteroid belt on its way to visit Vesta and Ceres in this artist's impression.

ASTEROIDS GALORE

The discovery of Ceres was the first in a wave of similar finds. In 1802 Heinrich Olbers of the Celestial Police spotted one close to Ceres and called it Pallas. Karl Harding discovered a third, named Juno, in 1804, and Olbers followed with a fourth, Vesta, in 1807. Vesta is not the largest asteroid, but it is the brightest and can be spotted with the naked eye in a clear dark sky. William Herschel coined the term asteroids, meaning "starlike," as astronomers realized that these were too small to be regular planets.

It took 38 years before another asteroid was found. The numbers logged since have run well beyond 400,000, but astronomers believe there are millions still waiting to be discovered. More than 200 already known are bigger than 60 miles (100 km) across, and latest estimates suggest that between 1.1 and 1.9 million could be three-fifths of a mile (1 km) or more wide. Jupiter's pull condemned these fragments to circle the Sun independently instead of joining to form a planet. In 1866 U.S. professor Daniel Kirkwood discovered that Jupiter's influence also left empty spaces in the asteroid belt, which are known as Kirkwood Gaps. There are also clumps of asteroids, called Trojans, locked in positions relative to certain planets.

VIEWING CLOSE UP

At one time, astronomers could only estimate asteroids' sizes and shapes by noting their changing brightness as they rotated, timing their occasional passages in front of a star, or bouncing radar signals off them. But since 1991, space probes have visited a number of bodies and observed them close-up. First call was to Gaspra by the *Galileo* probe on its way to Jupiter, and subsequent flybys have been made of many others, all cratered, potato-shaped rocks. NASA's *NEAR Shoemaker* craft actually landed on one called Eros, and another NASA probe, *Dawn*, was launched in 2007 to visit Vesta and Ceres in 2011 and 2015.

"It has occurred to me several times that it might be something better than a comet."

—Giuseppe Piazzi,
WHO DISCOVERED THE
FIRST ASTEROID

IMPACTS ON EARTH

Earth is not a heavily cratered world like the Moon or Mercury—most of the evidence has been wiped away by weathering and geological activity. But more than 150 impact sites have been identified, the scars left by collisions with asteroids long ago. Astronomers now monitor potentially hazardous space rocks to try to avoid a future disaster.

> *"If humans one day become extinct from a catastrophic collision, there would be no greater tragedy in the history of life in the universe. Not because we lacked the brain power to protect ourselves but because we lacked the foresight."*
>
> —Neil deGrasse Tyson, director of the Hayden Planetarium, New York

ARIZONA METEOR CRATER

The best-known impact site is the Barringer Crater in Arizona. About 4,300 feet (1,300 m) wide and 575 feet (175 m) deep, it was blasted out of the ground about 50,000 years ago. But until the twentieth century it was thought to have been caused by a volcano, and debate raged for decades before a cosmic cause was agreed upon. It is named after Daniel Barringer, who originally suspected a meteorite impact and bought the mining rights in 1902, believing a large, profitable lump of iron lay buried. Nothing was found, because the asteroid had been vaporized in a huge explosion.

A rather imaginative impression of dinosaurs fleeing the inferno after an asteroid has collided with Earth.

DEATH OF THE DINOSAURS

About 65 million years ago a cataclysmic event caused the demise of the dinosaurs. Research by geologist Walter Alvarez in 1980 revealed that Earth is covered by a layer of the dense metal iridium, the signature of a devastating asteroid impact. The site of the crater has since been found in Mexico's Yucatan Peninsula. While many dinosaurs undoubtedly died in the impact, most perished as forest fires and clouds of dust blocked out the Sun, destroying the plants on which they fed. In 2007 U.S. and Czech scientists using a computer model traced the deadly missile's origins back to a collision in the asteroid belt 160 million years ago.

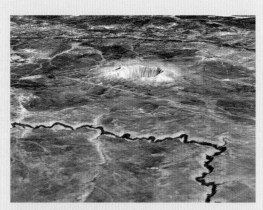

A view of the Barringer meteor crater in Arizona, which was identified as an impact site a century ago.

THE TUNGUSKA EVENT

Collisions are rarer in the solar system today than they once were, but a reminder of the danger they pose came in June 1908 when there was a huge explosion above a remote and, thankfully, sparsely inhabited region of Russia called Tunguska. It flattened 80 million trees over 770 square miles (2,000 sq km), but the only human casualty was a barrel maker knocked out by the blast. Experts believe a small asteroid, perhaps 35 miles (60 km) wide, blew up with the force of a 20-megaton nuclear device. No trace of the asteroid has been found, but similar airbursts have been detected since.

APOPHIS APPROACHES

New asteroids crossing our orbit are discovered on a regular basis, sparking the occasional scare story in the media. Most belong to a group called the Apollo asteroids. Usually the alerts turn out to be false alarms, because the asteroids' actual paths are refined to reveal that they pose no threat. An impact with one asteroid, Apophis—which is a quarter-mile (350 m) wide—in 2036 has still not been ruled out, though it's highly unlikely. Apophis will pass very close in 2029, at which point Earth's pull could affect its orbit. The tiny risk has prompted space agencies and others to consider special missions to deflect Apophis from its path.

MONITORING THE RISK

Asteroids more than 3 miles (5 km) wide probably strike Earth only once every 10 million years. Rocks more than 160 feet (50 m) wide, which could produce tsunamis and local disasters, may hit us once in a thousand years. But there is no regular pattern, and astronomers have begun searches using robotic telescopes to find and track asteroids, termed Potentially Hazardous Objects (PHOs), that could threaten us. Of more than 5,000 asteroids that approach Earth's orbit, fewer than a thousand are considered PHOs. It is estimated that 80 percent of near-Earth asteroids more than 0.62 miles (1 km) wide have been found, with about 200 yet to be discovered.

Many years after the impact that struck remote Tunguska in Russia, a photograph records the flattening of trees for hundreds of square miles.

STONES FROM THE SKY

A meteorite is a piece of space rock that has survived a fall through Earth's atmosphere. It arrives as a brilliant fireball, perhaps shining even brighter than the Moon. Meteorites are not generally related to the dust grains that produce shooting stars, but instead are mainly minor fragments produced when collisions occur in the asteroid belt.

A tenth-century depiction by Beatus from northern Spain of stars falling from the heavens in the apocalypse.

MYSTERY ROCKS

Before the Renaissance, it was accepted that stones could fall from the sky. But as science advanced, such ideas were regarded as superstitious nonsense. Chemical analysis in the early nineteenth century finally persuaded scientists that meteorites were stones from the sky, though it was wrongly imagined that they might have been fired out of lunar volcanoes.

ENSISHEIM

In 1492 a spectacular fireball over Ensisheim, in the Alsace region of France, was witnessed by a young boy. He found the meteorite, weighing about 330 pounds (150 kg), in a wheat field. Locals chipped bits off as good-luck charms before officials stopped them. King Maximilian of Austria took the fall as a divine sign that he could attack France, and he conquered three provinces. The meteorite—the oldest preserved and largest found in Europe—was chained up in a dungeon so that it could not fly away again. Today it can be seen in the town museum.

Confirmation that meteorites originated in space came when a shower of nearly 3,000 stones fell over L'Aigle, a town 80 miles (130 km) west of Paris, in April 1803. Investigators noted the lack of volcanoes in the area and found the stones contained nickel, as had other rocks from the sky. It was not until the late twentieth century, however, that comparison of these stones with material found around impact sites established the link between meteorites and asteroid collisions.

WHAT METEORITES ARE MADE OF

The analysis of meteorites tells us what asteroids are made of. More than three-quarters are carbonaceous—very dark chunks of material almost unchanged since the solar system was formed. Much rarer are the iron meteorites that are thought to be fragments from the cores of large asteroids that were broken up. A little under a fifth of meteorites are a stony-iron mix. Some meteorites found on Earth have been discovered to be pieces of the Moon, or Mars, ejected into space by asteroid impacts.

METEOROIDS AND METEORITES

A space rock becomes known as a meteorite only when it reaches the ground. Before that it is a meteoroid. Entering the atmosphere, the meteoroid becomes red hot on the outside, producing a black fusion crust. The interior remains intact, however, leaving the evidence of its origin. Contrary to popular belief, it is cold

A METEORITE'S PATH

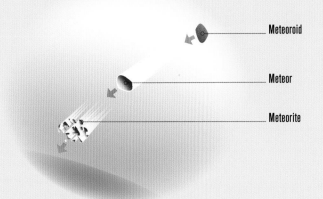

Meteoroid

Meteor

Meteorite

As a meteorite enters the atmosphere at high velocity it becomes extremely hot on the outside. Molten pieces and very hot gas break away to form a streak of bright light in the sky.

when landing. From the moment they were produced in an asteroid collision, meteoroids have been bombarded by cosmic rays. This radiation from deep in the universe leaves a signature in the stones that can be measured, allowing astronomers to tell the objects' age.

METEORITE INJURIES

The only confirmed incidence of someone being struck by a meteorite happened in November 1954, when a meteorite smashed through the roof in Sylacauga, Alabama. It struck Ann Hodges, badly bruising her leg. There are claims that a dog was killed during a shower of 40 meteorites over the village of Nakhla, Egypt, in 1911. Interestingly, 70 years later the meteorites were identified as having come from Mars.

A meteorite found in Antarctica in 1981 was found to be part of the moon, because it is almost identical to rocks brought back by *Apollo* astronauts.

CHAPTER THIRTEEN

COMETS AND METEORS

The graceful movements of the heavens are occasionally interrupted by the arrival of an unexpected celestial visitor called a comet. Though most are faint, such interlopers can make extremely dramatic entrances, and they were regarded as highly unwelcome portents of doom by the ancients.

Despite their sometimes spectacular appearance, with their glowing tails stretching across the sky, comets are, in reality, fairly insubstantial bodies. These tails are formed when the comet ejects gas and dust as it is warmed by the Sun's heat. Scientists find comets especially interesting since they contain material that has remained unchanged since the beginnings of the solar system.

When a particle no bigger than a grain of sand enters Earth's atmosphere, it is vaporized in a bright streak of light, and this is known as a meteor or shooting star. Every year Earth crosses several rivers of dust left by comets, causing meteor showers to occur. Very occasionally we pass through a particularly dense patch of dust, sparking a meteor storm. In recent years astronomers have begun to map the distribution of dust with greater precision.

WHAT WE KNEW THEN

Early people believed comets were warnings of death and destruction. Pliny the Elder even believed you could predict the type of impending disaster from the shape of the comet's tail.

WHAT WE THINK WE KNOW NOW

A comet is a collection of dust, rock, and ice from the outer reaches of the solar system, far beyond Pluto. It is believed that there is a vast cloud of billions of such bodies, some of which occasionally get diverted inward, carrying deep-frozen secrets from the formative period of the solar system.

Gas and dust erupt from a comet's nucleus, warmed by the Sun as it travels from the depths of space into the inner solar system.

"When beggars die, there are no comets seen;
The heavens themselves blaze forth the death of princes."

—WILLIAM SHAKESPEARE, "JULIUS CAESAR"

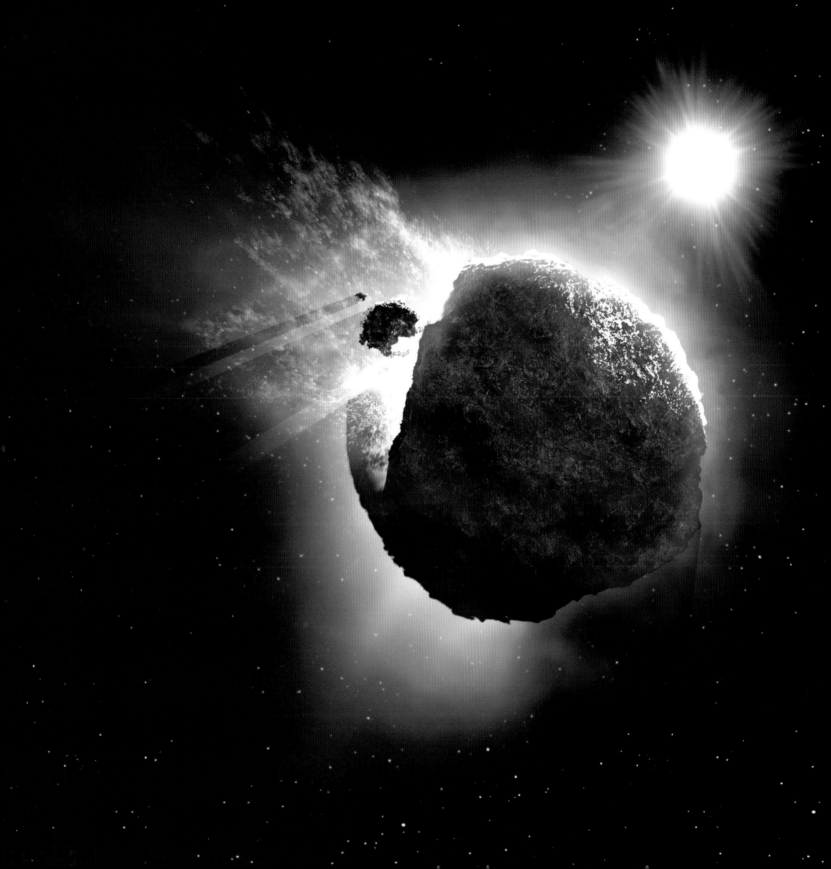

WHAT IS A COMET?

A comet can be one of the most spectacular objects in the heavens. Bright visitors have been spectacular sights in history when light pollution was not a problem, and the very greatest can still inspire awe—and even panic—today in our much-less-perfect skies.

Early representations of the tails of comets from the Mawangdui silk, compiled by the Chinese in about 300 B.C.

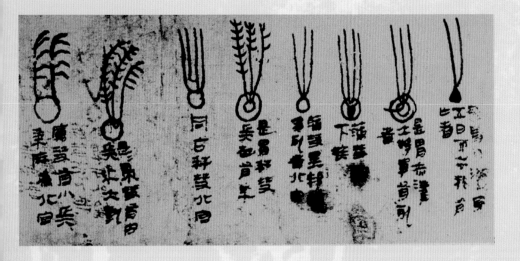

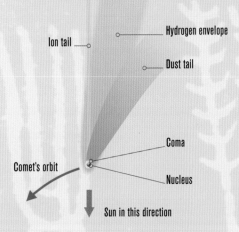

A COMET'S TAIL

Ion tail

Hydrogen envelope

Dust tail

Coma

Comet's orbit

Nucleus

Sun in this direction

A HEAD START

The icy ball that produces a comet is usually no more than a few tens of miles across. Called the nucleus, this is only visible as a starlike point in a telescope. As a comet approaches the inner solar system in an extremely extended orbit, the Sun's warmth thaws the ice, which causes gases to evaporate and expand into a ghostly head thousands of miles wide, called a coma. Only the more active comets form tails, and there are two types: a relatively straight gas tail that shows blue in photographs, and a curved tail of dust that can appear reddish.

SCIENCE FRICTION

In about 500 B.C., some Greek philosophers thought comets were produced when stars or planets ventured too close to one another. A century and a half later, Aristotle believed that comets and meteors were caused by friction in the upper air as the celestial sphere rotated. Comets were not recognized as related to the planets because they do not follow the zodiac and can arrive from any direction across the sky. Today we know that they originate either from the Kuiper Belt beyond Neptune or the Oort Cloud, a spherical reservoir of icy objects surrounding the solar system and nearly a light year away from the Sun.

THEREBY HANGS A TAIL

How comets' tails appear to us partly depends on the angle at which we view them. The Chinese kept records of them as early as the eighth century B.C., and they noted three main types of tail: bushy stars, broom stars, and long stars. The Chinese were also the first to note that the tails of comets always point away from the sun. We now know that this characteristic is caused by the force of the radiation stream from the sun. In 2007 a blast of this solar wind was so great that the tail of a frequent visitor, Comet Encke, became completely detached and blew away.

COMET HUNTING

Traditionally, comets have been named after their discoverers, and there has been fierce competition all around the world between dedicated amateur astronomers, who spend hours scouring the skies for the first hint of a fuzzy new arrival. In recent years robotic observatories making nightly surveys of the sky to discover potentially hazardous asteroids have begun mopping up a lot of new comets, too, making the challenge tougher for amateurs. Some astronomers are now building up tallies of new comets in a novel way, by examining archives of images from the SOHO satellite for any sign of a comet rounding the sun.

DAYLIGHT COMET

The most spectacular comet of recent years was first spotted in August 2006 by British astronomer Robert McNaught on a photographic image taken at Siding Spring Observatory in Australia. By January 2007 the comet had developed a fine tail that was visible to the unaided eye in the Northern Hemisphere, and it astonished observers by becoming bright enough to be seen in daylight as it rounded the sun in the middle of January. It then became a dazzling object for southern observers. Its dust tail was so long and broad that it could be detected from the Northern Hemisphere even when the comet's head lay below the horizon.

Comet McNaught was a stunning and unexpected visitor to the inner solar system in 2007, with a complex tail that stretched far across the sky.

THE ROVER'S RETURN

Many comets, including the brightest, are being documented for the first time because they can take many thousands of years to complete one trip around the Sun from the depths of space. Some are seen regularly, however, because they were diverted into smaller orbits by the planets, particularly giant Jupiter. The brightest of these is Halley's Comet.

Halley's Comet is recorded on the Bayeux Tapestry, which describes the events surrounding the Norman invasion of England in 1066. It was seen as an omen on the eve of the Battle of Hastings in England.

"I came in with Halley's Comet in 1835. It is coming again next year [1910], and I expect to go out with it."

—MARK TWAIN
(BORN WHEN HALLEY'S COMET VISITED IN 1835; DIED THE DAY AFTER IT WAS CLOSEST TO THE SUN ON ITS 1910 APPEARANCE)

HALLEY'S COMET

Halley's Comet is named not after any discoverer but after the English astronomer Edmond Halley, who first realized that a comet seen recurrently through history was one and the same, so he predicted its return in 1758. The comet comes round every 75 years 4 months and will return next in 2061. Recorded sightings go back to 240 B.C., when Chinese astrologers linked it to the deaths of two important figures. It also features on the eleventh-century Bayeux Tapestry, clearly alarming a huddle of pointing onlookers on the eve of the Battle of Hastings in 1066.

Comets such as Halley's travel in highly elongated, elliptical orbits. Johannes Kepler believed, like others before him, that comets moved in straight lines, so he did not apply his famous laws of planetary motion to them. In fact, they obey the law perfectly. When closest to the Sun, Halley moves at 34 miles per second (55 km/second), but its speed slows to about 0.5 miles per second (1 km/second) when out beyond Neptune.

PILLS AND PORTENTS

Bright comets can still inspire fear and alarm. When Halley's Comet returned in 1910, astronomers noted that Earth would pass through its tenuous tail, which was then known to contain the poisonous gas cyanogen. There could be no effect on our atmosphere, but that did not stop unscrupulous opportunists from selling special "comet pills" to the gullible. Comet Hale-Bopp, a brilliant visitor in 1997, sparked end-of-the-world warnings plus tragedy when 39 members of a California cult committed mass suicide, believing that their souls would be carried away by an imaginary spaceship accompanying the comet.

Comet Hale-Bopp in 1997 over Stonehenge, one of the few structures on Earth that would have existed when it last flew by.

EXPLORING COMETS

Comets have been visiting us throughout the life of the solar system, but in recent years we have started to visit them. The 1986 return of Halley's Comet was marked by the sending of a flotilla of five spacecraft—two Soviet, two Japanese, and one European. Of these, Europe's *Giotto* probe flew within 360 miles (580 km) of Halley's nucleus, giving us our first cometary close-up. In 2001 NASA's *Deep Space 1* zipped past Comet Borrelly, and in 2004 the *Stardust* probe flew through the coma of Comet Wild 2, collecting millions of particles that it delivered back to Earth in a canister as it flew past two years later.

NASA's *Deep Impact* probe attacked Comet Tempel 1 with a missile on July 4, 2005. The event was intended to reveal what lay within, but the explosion was so great that it obscured the view—though the flare from the cratered, potato-shaped comet was watched by telescopes on Earth. *Deep Impact* was intended to intercept a second comet, Boethin, but astronomers lost the target, which may have broken up. Instead, it will fly past Comet Hartley 2 in October 2010, but without any fireworks this time. A European Space Agency probe, *Rosetta*, will rendezvous with Comet Churyumov-Gerasimenko in 2014 to deposit a lander, Philae, on its surface.

HEAVY BOMBARDMENT

Chinese stargazers saw comets as "hairy stars" and watched them in wonder. Modern astronomers are fascinated by them because they are cosmic time capsules carrying material from the birth of the solar system. Analysis has shown that their chemistry is organic—including water ice, methane, and carbon compounds—beneath a sooty crust. Early in the solar system's life, when debris was flying all over the place, the planets suffered regular heavy bombardment by comets and asteroids. Indeed, some suggest that all the water in our oceans was dumped on us by comets and that, far from being omens of death, they actually brought the seeds of life to Earth.

DRAMATIC THAW

In 1950 the U.S. comet expert Fred Whipple proposed that comets were "dirty snowballs"—tightly packed bodies of ice and gravel. Our close-up images have refined this to reveal cratered crusts from which thawing jets of gas spew under enormous pressure. Faint comets sometimes undergo very rapid brightening as a result of such eruptions. In a particularly dramatic example in 2007, the normally faint Comet Holmes became half a million times brighter in just hours. The flare expanded into a ghostly ball that was visible to the naked eye for several weeks. This comet has form, though, because a similar flaring in 1892 led to its discovery.

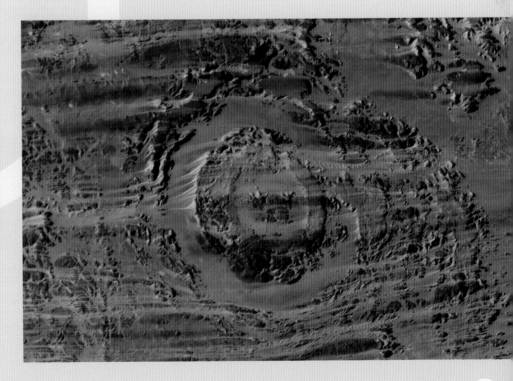

A photograph from space of the Sahara desert in northern Chad reveals the 10-mile (16-km) wide scar from an impact by a comet or asteroid hundreds of millions of years ago.

CELESTIAL FIREWORKS

A fanciful depiction of a meteor shower on a collectible cigarette card published around 1900.

"I would rather be a superb meteor, every atom of me in magnificent glow, than a sleepy and permanent planet."

—JACK LONDON, AUTHOR

Meteors are our closest contact with the universe beyond the Earth. Every clear night they may be seen as shooting stars streaking across the sky. In ancient times people thought they were just another phenomenon of the weather, like thunder and lightning. It was less than 300 years ago that some began to wonder whether they might have a celestial origin.

WHAT IS A METEOR?

A meteor appears when a tiny particle of rock—usually no larger than a grain of sand and as crumbly as an instant-coffee granule—speeds from space into our atmosphere at up to 43 miles per second (70 km/second). The air pressure causes the particle, called a meteoroid, to heat up and vaporize more than 40 miles (60 km) above the ground. The meteor itself is the streak of light caused by an effect called ionization on the molecules of air. Fittingly, the word "meteor" was Greek for "high in the air." A very bright meteor is known as a fireball, but even these generally burn up completely and do not reach the Earth.

WHERE METEORS COME FROM

Experts estimate that roughly 100 million meteors, bright enough to be seen with the naked eye, appear over the Earth every day. These natural fireworks must have presented a wondrous sight for many thousands of years; but, though there are records of particularly special displays stretching back centuries, no systematic observations were made until the eighteenth century. Studies showed that meteors were seen in greater abundance at

This nineteenth-century woodcut imagines the Leonid meteor storm of 1833. In reality, the radiant would have been much lower in the sky.

certain times of year than at others, which is when we get showers. The historical accounts record rare nights when it must have seemed as if the stars were falling from the heavens. Such events are called meteor storms.

STORMY WEATHER

In November 1799 a dramatic storm of shooting stars was witnessed from multiple sites around the world. Explorers visiting South America discovered that similar displays had been seen at roughly 30-year intervals. Furthermore, the meteors' tracks could all be traced back to the same region of the sky. This was the first understanding of the idea of a meteor radiant. As if on cue, there was a similar storm in 1833 and again in 1866. These meteors are known as the Leonids because they appear to radiate from Leo, and they have occurred at roughly 33-year intervals since. Following the latest major return in 1999 Leonid rates remained high in 2001 and 2002 but then declined once more.

DEATH OF A COMET

Biela's Comet was a short-period comet that returned at 6.6-year intervals during the nineteenth century. In 1846 it was seen to have split into two, and the fragments were once more seen, widely separated, in 1852. The comet was not seen again, but instead a meteor storm occurred in 1872 when Earth crossed its predicted path.

A brilliant Leonid fireball captured close to the stars of Leo in November 1999.

REGULAR SHOWERS

As meteor astronomy progressed, it was noted that other meteor showers happened at regular times each year. Today we know of several, and dedicated amateur astronomers make counts of them each time they return. Like the Leonids, the showers are named after the constellation from which they radiate, such as the Perseids from Perseus in July and August and the Geminids from Gemini in December. The effect is one of perspective. The meteoroids stream into the atmosphere in parallel flight but appear to diverge as they come closer to Earth, just as railway tracks seem to converge into the distance. At best, an individual observer watching the Perseids might see 50 or 60 an hour. Random meteors not linked to known showers are called sporadics.

MAPPING METEORS

Visual and photographic plotting of individual meteors' paths has allowed their orbits to be determined, and during the twentieth century the link between meteor streams and comets became increasingly clear. Building on the observations of amateurs since the nineteenth century, professional astronomers have recently been able to map some rivers of dust spread along cometary orbits with remarkable precision. This allows accurate forecasts of when individual showers will reach their peak. Earth crosses the trail of debris from Halley's Comet twice each year, producing the Eta Aquarid shower in May, and the Orionids in October.

CHAPTER FOURTEEN

EXTRASOLAR PLANETS

Centuries of study have greatly enhanced our knowledge and understanding of our own solar system. But in these early years of a new millennium, we are discovering that there are other solar systems that we have yet to explore. Humankind has long wondered whether we were alone in the universe. And now science is teaching us not only that our solar system is not unique, but also that families of planets could be the rule rather than the exception throughout the universe. In less than 20 years since the first planet was found around another star, many hundreds have been recorded, using a variety of detectors. Planet hunting is occupying the time of astronomers around the world, and the Holy Grail they seek is a planet like our own that might be home to intelligent life.

Our knowledge of these new worlds is doubtless as scant as that of Tycho, Kepler, or Galileo about the planets in our own family of worlds. However, the wisdom that today's scientists have gained by standing on the shoulders of such giants is allowing us to discover more and more about this amazing assortment of alien planets.

WHAT WE KNEW THEN

Our solar system's planets—then including Pluto—were the full extent of the worlds known to humankind for most of the last century. Astronomers could only speculate about whether or not there were other "Earths" in the universe, and the possibility of alien civilizations was just a fantasy.

WHAT WE THINK WE KNOW NOW

Observatories on Earth and in space have begun harvesting a host of new worlds that are once more altering our understanding of our cosmic environment. These new kids on the block are termed extrasolar planets—or exoplanets, for short—and they open up the possibility once more that we are not alone.

"The great ocean of truth lay all undiscovered before me."

—Sir Isaac Newton

Giant worlds many times the size of Jupiter are being found around other stars, leading astronomers to believe there might be Earthlike planets, too.

THE QUEST FOR OTHER WORLDS

The first planets to be found outside our own solar system were not discovered until the tail end of the twentieth century. Since then there has been a flurry of finds—the number runs into hundreds. It has become clear that our solar system is by no means unique.

BRUNO THE BRAVE

Giordano Bruno was an Italian friar who traveled Europe in the sixteenth century, outraging the Church and the establishment with the zany concepts that he preached. Bruno embraced Copernicus's model of the universe, but he went even further. He believed that planets surrounded all stars, not just the Sun, and that they were probably all inhabited. He was not an astronomer and was drawn to Copernicus only because his teachings fitted with his own imaginings. But there is no doubting his bravery. After years of imprisonment, he was burned at the stake in Rome, refusing to recant his views.

Auroras dance around the pole of one of the planets orbiting an exotic pulsar in Virgo.

A LIGHT WOBBLE

The quest for planets around other stars began more than 50 years ago. There were a number of false alarms in the 1950s and 1960s, when astronomers reported tiny wobbles in the light of some stars that they thought were caused by the pull of invisible planets orbiting them. Though this *is* a valid way to detect extrasolar planets, the wobbles would have been too tiny to be detected by the earthbound telescope technology then in use.

PULSAR PLANETS

The first real planets were detected in 1992, not around an ordinary star, but orbiting a pulsar—the superdense neutron star formed when the core of a supernova collapses. The pulsar—980 light years away in Virgo—had= only itself been discovered two years previously by Polish professor Aleksander Wolszczan, and given the label PSR B1257+12. An investigation into the erratic nature of its pulses, using the world's largest radio telescope at Arecibo in Puerto Rico, revealed the presence of two planets. A third was later confirmed as well as another object that could be a comet or asteroid.

WORLDS OFF THE PEG

In 1995 a planet was at last found orbiting a normal star, more like our own Sun. The star, just visible to the naked eye in Pegasus, is

known as 51 Peg and lies about 50 light years away. Swiss astronomers Michel Mayor and Didier Queloz, working at the Haute-Provence Observatory in France, noticed changes in the spectrum of the star's light, indicating that there was an object orbiting it. Additional analysis showed that the planet, nicknamed Bellerophon, was nearer in size to Jupiter than Earth, but it was closer to its parent star than Mercury is to the Sun, whizzing around it in little over four days. Subsequent finds have revealed that these "hot Jupiters" are common around other stars. By mid 2008 more than 300 planets had been found in other solar systems, the majority of them fast-moving gas giants.

LUCKY DIPS

One method for detecting planets is to monitor stars for transits as a planet passes in front of them. An invisible world reveals its presence by causing a very slight drop in the star's brightness. Robotic cameras are scanning large areas of the sky every night to watch for these almost imperceptible dips, with much success. However, this method works only for planets with orbits edge-on to us. Another technique involves gravitational lensing, where a distant star's light is slightly bent by the pull of another star between it and the observer. If the foreground star has a planet, causing it to wobble, this affects the appearance of the more distant star.

An impression of a "hot Jupiter"—one of hundreds now discovered—zipping around another star.

"It's the first step in man's quest to find life elsewhere."

—BILL BORUCKI,
PRINCIPAL INVESTIGATOR
FOR THE KEPLER MISSION

There has been great success with a British project called SuperWASP, which operates banks of powerful cameras at sites in the Canary Islands and South Africa. Each robotic observatory uses eight telephoto lenses to monitor thousands of stars every night for flickers in their light caused by transiting giant planets.

IS THERE ANYBODY OUT THERE?

Tracking the orbits of giant planets around other stars led scientists to believe that there must be smaller worlds, too. As search techniques become more sophisticated, rocky worlds more like Earth are finally being identified. Scientists are searching for signs that some might be habitable—and even for signals from the aliens themselves.

An imagined view of planets orbiting the red dwarf star Gliese 581, including one in the so-called Goldilocks zone.

THE GOLDILOCKS ZONE

Astronomers are especially eager to find planets in the region around stars similar to that occupied by the Earth around the Sun, where rocky worlds can exist with water and other suitable conditions for life. This habitable region has been dubbed the Goldilocks Zone because, like her porridge, it is "just right." In 2007, one planet fitting the bill was detected orbiting a red-dwarf star called Gliese 581 in Libra. Other candidates include a world that is one of five planets detected around a sunlike star called 55 Cancri, 41 light years away in Cancer. And, in June 2008, astronomers in Chile reported finding three planets, all with less than 10 times the Earth's mass, around a planet 42 light years away in Pictor.

DUST THE JOB

Besides planets, astronomers are finding evidence of dusty disks around some stars that appear to resemble the zone of debris that collected to form our own solar system billions of years ago. Heat-seeking telescopes in space, which observe with infrared eyes, are particularly suited to finding these. Watching

Light from the star Beta Pictoris is masked to reveal that it is encircled by two dusty disks, one inclined toward the other in this image from the Hubble space telescope.

brightness changes in starlight has also allowed one such telescope, NASA's Spitzer, to map the surface brightness of larger Jupiter-like planets, discover whether they have atmospheres and what gases they contain, and even check for windy weather. A more powerful instrument, NASA's James Webb space telescope, due for launch in 2013, is expected to be able to capture details on earthlike worlds, too.

SO WHERE ARE THEY?

The actual hunt for any sign of alien presence is called SETI—the Search for Extra-Terrestrial Intelligence. It was begun by U.S. radio-astronomer Frank Drake in 1960, when he used a radio telescope at Green Bank, West Virginia, to listen for any signals from two nearby stars, Tau Ceti and Epsilon Eridani, that resemble the Sun. Nothing was found.

Of the projects initiated since then, the one that has most gripped the public imagination is one launched in 1999 called SETI@home, which allows anyone with a computer to take part. All they have to do is download a program that runs automatically in the background, analyzing a chunk of radio data received from space. When that data has been examined for any signs of intelligence, the results are sent back to the organizers over the Internet and a fresh chunk of data is downloaded for analysis. By early 2008 more than 5 million computer users had signed up to take part—but that tantalizing alien broadcast is still awaited.

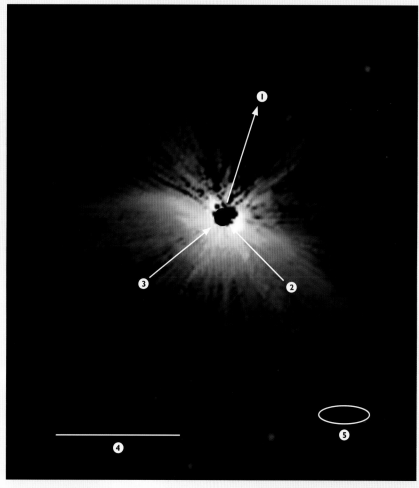

SEARCHING FROM SPACE

Searching for extrasolar planets is a major part of the mission for Europe's *Corot* satellite, launched in 2006. It is scanning stars for transit-type fades. A similar NASA mission, called *Kepler*, is due for launch in 2009, and others are planned for the following decade.

A giant moth in space, with a wingspan of 22 billion miles (35.4 billion km), is a disk of dust around the nearby young star HD 61005.

❶ Direction of star's motion

❷ Position of star

❸ Mask to hide star's glare

❹ 150 AU

❺ Size of Neptune's orbit

CHAPTER FIFTEEN

OBSERVING THE PLANETS

Reading about the solar system is one thing, but seeing the planets for yourself is a must-do experience. Ancient man must have had his attention distracted regularly by the brilliant lights of Venus, Mars, Jupiter, and Saturn. These days, when street lamps render these planets' beams more feeble and television is the major distraction in our lives, many people can go through life without ever recognizing a planet at all. Even the Moon is taken for granted and rarely given a second glance.

If you have never seen a bright planet, it is well worth making the effort. You will not need a telescope for the bright four, or for Mercury if you are able to catch one of its fleeting appearances before dawn or after sunset. Once you have logged those, you might even try for Uranus and Neptune. Discover them for yourself and enjoy a taste of what it must have been like for those who gazed upon them for the first time. It can be a great andidote to the stresses of modern life, and it will give you sense of our place in the universe.

*"Astronomy compels the soul
to look upward, and leads us from
this world to another."*

—PLATO

WHAT WE KNEW THEN

Just a few years ago, amateur astronomers had to brave cold nights. They often observed through home-made telescopes because of the prohibitive -cost of commercially produced instruments. A trained eye was required to sketch planetary markings—cameras were bulky and used photographic plates too slow to capture much detail.

WHAT WE THINK WE KNOW NOW

Today's astronomer with a little bit of cash to spend can sit indoors in the warmth, remotely monitoring the view through a computer-controlled telescope. Global Postioning System—SatNav—tells the telescope its location so that it can automatically find a target, and sensitive CCD (charge-coupled device) cameras record detailed features that the eye may not quite perceive.

An amateur astronomer gets set for a night's observing under crystal clear skies at a dark location well away from any light pollution.

USING YOUR PLANISPHERE

The planisphere that comes with this book will help you dial up the sky as it appears over your backyard. The lower disk is printed with the bright stars that can be seen from your part of the world over the course of the year. The transparent oval on the overlay is like a window on this star chart, and it can be turned to show the stars in your sky at any time of the night—or day, actually, because they are there even if you cannot see them.

A PLANISPHERE

The outer band on the base of the planisphere shows the days and months of the year.

The inner ring printed on the upper disk shows the hours and minutes of the day. Turn this to align your time with your date.

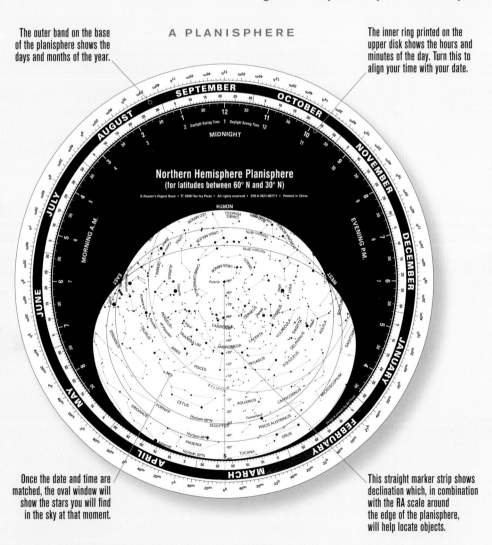

Once the date and time are matched, the oval window will show the stars you will find in the sky at that moment.

This straight marker strip shows declination which, in combination with the RA scale around the edge of the planisphere, will help locate objects.

DIALING THE SKY

Around the edge of your planisphere's disk are the months and days of the month. The inner dial shows the time. Turn this dial until the time you want is lined up against the date required. The stars in the window will be the stars in the sky at that time. If your region is using Daylight Saving Time, you should subtract an hour to obtain a more accurate view.

The edge of the oval represents your horizon, and the center of the oval is the point overhead. Imagine holding the planisphere above you with the compass directions on the edge of the oval aligned with those directions on the ground.

The hours and minutes on the very edge of your planisphere should not be confused with the time. These are the measures of right ascension (RA) that are part of the grid of the celestial sphere. You can ignore them if you are just dialing up your sky. Otherwise, you can use this scale in combination with the straight strip marking degrees of declination (dec) to locate targets in the sky.

You will notice that the window shows more than one oval shape. This is to allow for the slightly different view you get from different latitudes in your hemisphere.

POSITIONS IN THE SKY

As described on page 14, astronomers use a grid measuring RA against dec to describe the position of an object in the sky. These two measurements equate to longitude and latitude on Earth and simply apply to a map of the heavens instead of a map of the world. They are treating the imaginary celestial sphere as we might the globe of the Earth, and the principle is the same even though we are viewing the dome of the sky from within.

RA is the equivalent of longitude and is normally described in hours, minutes, and seconds, from zero up to 24. Dec is described in degrees from zero to 90 on either side of the celestial equator, with negative numbers given to southern positions (for example, -40 degrees). The path of the ecliptic may be seen in blue, running through the constellations of the zodiac. You will always find the moon and planets close to this line.

UNDERSTANDING PRECESSION

The slow wobble of the Earth's axis—precession—means that the positions of the north and south celestial poles move gradually over time. This affects the whole RA–dec grid, though not the positions of the stars themselves, so astronomical cartographers tend to update their charts to fit epochs 50 years apart. However, the effects of precession are too slight over one lifetime to bother the individual observer much.

HOW A PLANISPHERE WORKS

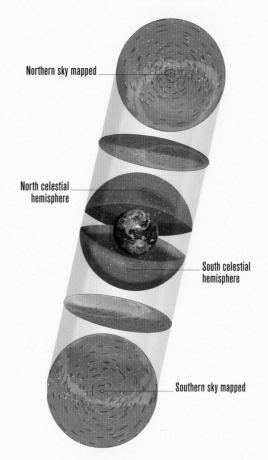

Northern sky mapped

North celestial hemisphere

South celestial hemisphere

Southern sky mapped

The stars of the celestial sphere are split into two hemispheres and flattened to produce maps of the northern and southern sky. These form the basis for planispheres for observers north or south of the equator, although each planisphere includes some overlap.

THE SKY DOME

From any point on Earth the stars and planets appear as if placed on half a sphere, like being inside a planetarium.

VISUAL AIDS

Stars are shown in different sizes to indicate their different brightnesses or magnitudes. In reality they will always appear as points of light, however bright they are, even through a telescope. The blue river crossing the background star map is a representation of the position of the edge of our galaxy, the Milky Way. It appears obvious in a clear, dark, moonless sky, but light pollution or a hazy sky will hide it.

SPOT THE PLANET

It is not possible to show the planets on your planisphere because they are always moving. But if you look up their positions with the help of this book (or perhaps an online guide), you can then check which planets are in your sky at any given time and date.

CHOOSING A TELESCOPE

There has never been a better time to buy a telescope, because the quality and value for your money have greatly improved in recent years. Telescopes on sale today, made with modern techniques and sold at relatively modest prices, will usually show you better images in greater detail than pioneers, such as Galileo, enjoyed.

A replica of Isaac Newton's original reflecting telescope, the model on which professional telescopes including Hubble are still based.

MOUNTING EXCITEMENT

Whichever type of telescope you choose, the mounting is as important as the optics. If your mount is flimsy and wobbles like Jell-O® in the slightest breeze, this movement will be greatly magnified when you try to view anything and make observing virtually impossible. Mounts come in two basic types: an equatorial mount, which you can line up with the Earth's axis, making it easier to follow an object as it crosses the sky; and an altazimuth, which moves horizontally and vertically. Both types now commonly come with GoTo computer controls to send your device automatically to observing targets.

ADVANCES IN OPTICS

There are two main types of telescope, the refractor and the reflector, but plenty of variations on these themes. The refractor was the simple arrangement of lenses that Galileo in Italy and Thomas Harriott in England employed to make the first telescopic observations of the heavens. The reflector uses mirrors to collect and direct the light, which is then magnified with an eyepiece. It was invented by all-around science genius Isaac Newton and used by William Herschel, discoverer of Uranus, among others. These early instruments appear remarkably crude today, and the optics were so small that they gathered little light from the targets being observed.

SEEING THE LIGHT

A basic refractor, or refracting telescope or refractor, collects an object's light with a large lens called an objective. A magnifying lens, called an eyepiece, is then used to magnify the image delivered by the main lens. In a modern telescope, a range of eyepieces may be used to give different powers of magnification. Objective lenses may be made with different curvatures to produce different focal lengths.

A large refractor is the favored instrument for the astronomer in nineteenth-century German artist Carl Spitzweg's painting, *The Stargazer.*

Generally, planets are better seen in telescopes with long focal lengths. Galileo's refractor used simple lenses, so it must have been affected by a phenomenon called chromatic aberration, which produced colorful fringes around objects being viewed. This occurs because glass refracts different colors to slightly different points. More expensive refracting telescopes can reduce this effect by using a combination of lenses.

ALL DONE WITH MIRRORS

Reflectors, or reflecting telescopes, come in various types derived from Newton's original. The classic Newtonian reflector uses a curved mirror, somewhat like a shaving mirror, to collect the light. It sends this light back up the tube to a small flat mirror, at a 45-degree angle, which directs it into the eyepiece in the side that focuses it. Again the main mirror's curvature determines the telescope's focal length, and the bigger this mirror, the more light is collected for magnification. Reflectors benefit from a lack of the color-fringing problems that can plague cheaper refractors. Popular models of commercial telescopes today combine elements from reflecting and refracting telescopes to produce optical designs that allow telescopes to be more compact but give better images.

WHICH TELESCOPE?

It is not always easy to gauge the quality of a telescope when you see it in a shop in daylight. If you can, try to look through a few instruments at a local astronomical society's observing session, or ask experienced members for advice. As a rule of thumb, go for as much aperture—the diameter of the objective lens or main mirror—as you can afford. A standard refractor with a 4-inch (10-cm) objective will offer good views, and a 6-inch (15-cm) one will be even better. A 6-inch (15-cm) mirror is really the minimum for a Newtonian reflector, but 8 inches (20 cm) is a popular standard. More compact telescopes, such as Meade's ETX90, offer good views with high-quality optics and long focal length, despite the smaller aperture. A bigger budget will pay for other features, such as a GPS built into the telescope to help locate objects in the sky for you.

BUYER BEWARE!
Beware of the really cheap telescopes seen in many newspaper advertisements or some catalogs—they promise much and deliver very little. A pair of binoculars is more useful if you are on a really tight budget.

A compact telescope with its own built-in computer drive uses a sophisticated optical assembly for more advanced amateur studies.

TOURING THE SOLAR SYSTEM

You do not need to fly into space to tour the solar system. You can follow the bright planets' paths or observe shooting stars with the naked eye, while telescopes will give close-up views of the moon and planets that are the next best thing to going there.

Citizens of Paris keep an eye out for a celestial event in a humorous illustration from Le Charivari in 1857.

MOPPING UP METEORS

A telescope is not required for observing meteors. Amateur astronomers sit out in lawnchairs under clear skies for periods of, perhaps, an hour at a time in order to count the meteors they observe streaking across the sky. This is most rewarding around the time of a major meteor shower—such as the Perseids, which peak in August—because of the greater numbers you will see. Astronomers a century ago used to mark meteors' paths on star charts, but photography has made this a mostly redundant exercise.

EYE VERSUS CAMERA

When you have found your planet in a telescope, don't put your eye to the eyepiece and expect to see much detail right away. It takes time for the eye to adjust and patience to see the subtle shadings that are there. If the atmosphere is not perfectly steady, you may find that good views last only a few fleeting moments. Sketching the features that you do see has been a popular pastime for amateurs, using ready-prepared forms supplied by major astronomical societies.

In recent years electronic imaging has become increasingly popular, using lightweight, highly sensitive charge-coupled device (CCD) cameras. Even webcams can produce surprisingly good results, especially when individual sharp frames are selected and combined to produce an enhanced picture. The best CCD images can reveal a level of detail that visual observers could never be able to sketch.

A sketch by Leonardo da Vinci who correctly deduced in the early sixteenth century that the dark region of a crescent moon is visible due to sunlight reflected from Earth.

VIEW TO A THRILL

Don't be surprised to find that the view through your telescope is upside down. This is usual with astronomical telescopes, since the extra lens required to give an upright image would cut out a little of the light from the object you are viewing. Therefore, you will often see astronomical photos displayed with south at the top.

HUNT THE COMET

The most dedicated amateur astronomers used to spend hours under the stars sweeping the sky with telescopes or large binoculars in the hope of finding a new comet—especially because of the tradition that new discoveries are given their finder's name. The growth of professional robotic cameras, which scour the skies for potentially hazardous asteroids, is now finding a lot of these cosmic visitors first, but finds are still being made by humans.

Venus's fragile crescent as it lies near its closest point to Earth is recorded by an amateur astronomer's CCD camera.

Modern CCD cameras allow amateurs to record subtle detail as in this exquisite image of Saturn.

POWER TO THE PEOPLE

Telescopes often come with a range of eyepieces with different focal lengths described in millimeters. Their actual magnification depends on the telescope, but the smaller the figure for the eyepiece, the higher the magnification will be. Resist the temptation to use the highest power. A lower magnification will make it easier to find your target, after which you can try other eyepieces. The highest powers are usually only usable on rare nights when turbulence in the atmosphere—known as seeing—is absent.

DIGITAL DESIGNS

Ordinary digital cameras have made it easy to take snapshots of the Moon. With care the camera can just be held to a telescope's eyepiece, but special clamps are available to make supporting the camera simple. You can also buy an adapter that attaches the body of a SLR (single-lens reflex) camera to a telescope, effectively making the instrument the camera's lens.

ALBEDO Measure of the reflective power of an otherwise non-luminous celestial body, defined as a percentage (the Moon's albedo = 0.07).

APHELION Farthest orbital distance from the Sun.

APOGEE Farthest orbital distance from the Earth.

APOLLO ASTEROID Asteroid of a group that occasionally penetrates the Earth's orbit.

ASTEROID Minor planet, generally orbiting between Mars and Jupiter.

ASTROMETRY Measurement of planetary and stellar positions.

ASTRONOMICAL UNIT Mean distance from the Earth to the Sun, used as a measurement (a.u. or AU) of distance in space.

AURORA Luminous display in the Earth's upper atmosphere at the far north or south, caused by the arrival there of charged particles from the Sun.

AZIMUTH Compass bearing of a celestial object measured in degrees clockwise from north.

BAILY'S BEADS Optical effect in the first and last moments of a total eclipse, as the edge of the Sun appears through the valleys and craters of the Moon.

BODE'S LAW Supposed mathematical relationship between the distances of the planets from the Sun.

BOLIDE Fiery meteor, particularly one that then explodes (also known as a detonating **FIREBALL**).

CELESTIAL SPHERE Huge, hypothetical, rotating sphere surrounding and concentric with the Earth, corresponding to the visible sky.

CHROMOSPHERE Dense, major layer of the Sun's atmosphere between the surface (**PHOTOSPHERE**) and the **CORONA**.

COMA (COMETARY) Bright, gaseous envelope that surrounds and streams out behind the nucleus of a comet passing the Sun.

COMET Relatively tiny planetoid in an eccentric orbit around the Sun.

CONJUNCTION Optical coming together of two celestial bodies.

CONSTELLATION Pattern perceived in a group of stars in the night sky.

CORONA Tenuous, hot outer layer of the Sun's atmosphere.

CORONAL MASS EJECTION Sudden emission from the solar corona of a plasma of atomic particles within a magnetic field.

COSMOLOGY Study of the nature, structure, and contents of the universe.

CRATER Bowl-shaped depression in the ground, sometimes with raised rim, caused by impact or explosion.

CUSP Point at top or bottom of a crescent moon; initial point of an astrological house.

DECLINATION Measurement in degrees of a celestial body north or south of the celestial equator.

ECCENTRICITY Measurable deviation from regularity or from comparative norm.

ECLIPSE Apparent passage of one celestial body in front of another that hides part or all of the body behind.

ECLIPTIC Apparent path of the Sun through the stars of the night sky over one year, effectively corresponding to the Earth's orbit.

ELLIPSE/ELLIPTICAL Regular oval; of geometrically regular oval form.

ELONGATION Measure in degrees between the apparent positions of a primary celestial body (like the Sun), and a secondary one (like a planet).

EQUINOX Either of two points in the year when the duration of day and night is precisely equal. For example, at which the ecliptic cuts the celestial equator.

ESCAPE VELOCITY Velocity at and above which it is possible to escape the pull of gravity.

FIREBALL Fiery meteor. *See also* **BOLIDE**.

FLARE Explosive release of energy in the upper atmosphere of the Sun (or another star), particularly in the area of a **SUNSPOT**.

GALAXY One of many vast but homogenous systems comprising stars, nebulae, and interstellar matter; the Milky Way galaxy is the one that contains our Sun.

GEOCENTRIC With the Earth at the center.

GRANULATION Formation and appearance of the Sun's "granular" photosphere, caused by convection currents in the plasma.

GREATEST ELONGATION Position of Mercury or Venus when farthest (at the greatest angle) from the Sun in the sky.

HELIOCENTRIC With the Sun at the center.

INCLINATION Measure in degrees of the angle between a plane of reference (such as the plane of the Earth's equator) and another plane (such as the plane of the Earth's orbit).

INFERIOR CONJUNCTION Position of Venus or Mercury when directly between the Earth and the Sun.

INFERIOR PLANET Planet nearer the Sun than Earth.

KEPLER'S LAWS Three laws "of planetary motion" (two about elliptical orbits, the third relating distance from the Sun to the planetary "year").

KIRKWOOD GAPS Gaps in the distribution of main-belt asteroids.

KUIPER BELT Belt of frozen, mainly gaseous planetary debris extending from the orbit of Neptune way beyond the main solar system; Pluto is the largest known member.

LIBRATION The slight turning back and forth of the Moon's face toward the Earth over time.

LIGHT YEAR Distance traveled by light in one Earth year: 5.87812 miles, 9.46012 km, 63,241 a.u., 0.3066 parsec.

LONG-PERIOD COMET Comet with an orbital period around the Sun of more than 200 years.

LUNAR LIMB A term to describe the edge of the visible surface of the Moon when viewed from Earth.

MAGNITUDE Apparent magnitude is the brightness of a celestial body, measured on a logarithmic scale as if seen with no intervening Earth's atmosphere; the absolute magnitude of a star is the apparent magnitude it would have if it were 10 parsecs away, and of a solar system **PLANET** or planetoid is the apparent magnitude it would have if it were 1 a.u. away from both the Sun and the Earth.

MARE Darker area otherwise known as "sea" or "ocean" on the Moon.

MERIDIAN Theoretical line round the circumference of the Earth through the poles; thus by extension, a line round the circumference of the celestial sphere through the **ZENITH** and both celestial poles.

METEOR Streak of light visible from the Earth's surface when a tiny particle of space debris enters and burns up in the Earth's atmosphere.

METEORITE Large, solid lump of space debris that is not totally destroyed when it penetrates the Earth's atmosphere, and may impact the surface.

METEOROID Particle of traveling space debris responsible for a **METEOR**.

MILKY WAY Our local galaxy, visible in the night sky as a distinct swathe of (relatively dim) stars.

MINOR PLANET Another name for an asteroid, but particularly for a large one.

MOON Planetary satellite; the Moon is the Earth's.

NADIR Point on the celestial sphere that is directly beneath the feet of the observer (and is thus the opposite of the **ZENITH**).

NEAR-EARTH OBJECT Any asteroid, comet or meteoroid the orbit of which takes it closer than 1.3 a.u. to the Earth's orbit.

NEBULA Enormous cloud of dust, gas and plasma "floating" in space.

NEW MOON Phase of the Moon at which it is not visible from the Earth.

NUCLEUS (COMETARY) Basic orbiting head or body of the comet, usually solid, but porous and containing frozen gases.

OCCULTATION Concealment of part or all of one celestial body by another that passes in front of it.

OORT CLOUD Hypothesized collection of cometary debris and planetoids lying nearly 1 light year from the Sun but from which some comets are thought to derive; it is thus held to be the boundary of the solar system.

OPPOSITION Position of a planet such that the Earth is directly between it and the Sun.

ORBIT Path of one celestial body around another under the effect of gravity; one revolution on that path.

ORRERY Mechanical model of the Sun and the planets capable of showing their relative movements.

PENUMBRA Area of less than full shadow; lighter part of a sunspot.

PERIGEE Closest orbital distance from the Earth.

PERIHELION Closest orbital distance from the Sun.

PERIODIC COMET Comet visible from the Earth at regular intervals.

PERTURBATION Wobble or deviation in an orbit caused by gravitational effects of other celestial bodies.

PHASES Recurring different visible aspects of a celestial body, particularly the Moon.

PHOTOSPHERE Granular surface of the Sun.

PLANET Major satellite orbiting a star.

PLANETARY NEBULA Small, dense, hot star enveloped in a gaseous shell.

PLANISPHERE Two-dimensional representation of the constellations on the celestial sphere, often related to the calendar year.

PLUTOID A new category of celestial body developed by the International Astronomical Union. to describe dwarf planets in orbit around the sun at a distance greater than that of Neptune.

POLAR CAP Areas of ice or other frozen material at the poles.

POTENTIALLY HAZARDOUS ASTEROID (PHA) Asteroid with an Earth minimum orbit intersection distance of 0.05 a.u. and an absolute magnitude of 22.0 or less.

PRECESSION Apparent movement over time of the celestial poles as perceived on the Earth.

PROMINENCE Mass of glowing gases (mostly hydrogen) rising from the Sun's **PHOTOSPHERE**.

PROPLYD Rotating disk-shaped formation of dense gases surrounding a star, especially one newly formed.

PROTOSTAR Mass of solid matter gradually condensing out of the gases in a molecular cloud in the interstellar medium.

QUADRATURE Position at right-angles to the Sun or the Moon or a planet, as perceived from the Earth.

RADIANT Point in the night sky from which a meteor shower seems to originate.

RADIATION PRESSURE Pressure exerted by electromagnetic radiation on a surface (which may absorb it or reflect it).

RAY CRATER Crater from the rim of which "streaks" of matter radiate outward as a result of the original impact.

RED DWARF Class of star in the main sequence that is small and comparatively cool; very common type.

RED GIANT Class of star that is large and luminous, but of comparatively low mass and low temperature as its energy dwindles.

RED SPOT Large, prominent, rolling oval feature in the South Tropical Zone of the upper atmosphere of Jupiter.

RETROGRADE MOTION Movement backward in orbit or rotation, especially in comparison with the Earth's orbit or rotation.

RIGHT ASCENSION (RA) Angular distance of a celestial body from the vernal equinox westward, generally measured as a time difference (in hours, minutes, and seconds) between the height above the horizon of the equinox and that of the celestial body.

RILLE Long, narrow valley on the surface of the Moon.

ROCHE LIMIT Distance from the gravitational "control" of our Sun.

SOLAR WIND Flow of charged atomic particles radiating from the Sun.

SUNSPOT Small, dark area on the Sun's surface (**PHOTOSPHERE**) representing a cooler region of intense magnetic activity.

SUPERIOR CONJUNCTION Position of Venus or Mercury when directly behind the Sun from the Earth.

SUPERIOR PLANET Planet farther than Earth from the Sun.

SYNCHRONOUS ORBIT Orbit around a primary body precisely equal in duration and direction to the primary body's own axial rotation.

SYNCHRONOUS ROTATION Rotation of an orbiting body precisely equal in duration and direction to the primary body's own axial rotation.

SYNODIC PERIOD Time for a superior planet between one **OPPOSITION** and another.

TEKTITE Small, dark, glassy nodule that may be meteoritic in origin.

TERRESTRIAL PLANET The Earth, or a planet like the Earth in density and overall composition.

TRANSIT Optical passage of an inferior planet across the face of the Sun.

TROJAN ASTEROID Any of two groups of asteroids that follow (in Lagrangian points) the orbital path of the planet Jupiter.

TROPIC Either of the two circles on the celestial sphere representing the farthest north or south of the equator (23½°) that the Sun reaches at summer and winter solstices.

UMBRA Full shadow; darker part of a sunspot.

UNIVERSE The totality of the contents of space.

VAN ALLEN BELTS Two toroidal systems of charged particles around the Earth, one inside the other, both trapped by the Earth's magnetic field.

VERNAL EQUINOX Point in the third week of March at which the ecliptic cuts the celestial equator and from which **RIGHT ASCENSION** is calculated.

ZENITH Point on the celestial sphere that is immediately above the observer, see also **NADIR**.

RESOURCES

SOCIETIES AND ORGANIZATIONS

IN THE UNITED STATES

Association of Lunar and Planetary Observers
alpo-astronomy.org
U.S. organization specializing in the observation of the solar system.

Astronomical Society of the Pacific
www.astrosociety.org
A leading society for U.S. stargazers.

IN THE UNITED KINGDOM

British Astronomical Association
britastro.org
U.K. organization for advanced amateur astronomers.

Society for Popular Astronomy
www.popastro.com
U.K. society aimed at beginners. It has a special "Young Stargazers" section for the under-16 set.

IN CANADA

Royal Astronomical Society of Canada
www.rasc.ca
For amateur and professional astronomers in Canada.

IN AUSTRALIA AND NEW ZEALAND

Astronomical Society of Australia
www.astronomy.org.au
Societies in Australia tend to be very regional but you can find a list in the amateur section of this site.

Royal Astronomical Society of New Zealand

www.rasnz.org.nz
Leading society for astronomers.

INTERNATIONAL

Astronomical Society of Southern Africa
www.saao.ac.za/assa

The Planetary Society
www.planetary.org
An international organization promoting exploration of the planets.

WEBSITES

www.calsky.com
Very useful site for locating the planets and their orientation at any time.

www.esa.int
Information about European space research.

www.nasa.gov
News, images, and information about U.S. missions to the planets.

SOFTWARE

Stellarium—a free, open-source computer planetarium program for Mac OS X, Windows, and Linux systems.
www.stellarium.org

BOOKS

The Cambridge Guide to the Solar System
Kenneth R. Lang
(Cambridge University Press, 2003)

Collins Stars and Planets Guide
Heather Couper and Nigel Henbest
(Collins, 2007)

The Compact NASA Atlas of the Solar System
Ronald Greeley and Raymond Batson
(Cambridge University Press, 2001)

The History of Astronomy
Ian Ridpath
(Firefly, 2007)

An Introduction to the Solar System
Neil McBride, Iain Gilmour
(Cambridge University Press, 2004)

The New Solar System
J. Kelly Beatty, Carolyn Collins Petersen, Andrew L. Chaikin (author)
(Cambridge University Press, 1998)

Observing the Moon: The Modern Astronomer's Guide
Gerald North
(Cambridge University Press, 2007)

Philip's Solar System Observer's Guide
Peter Grego
(Philips, 2005)

The Planets
David McNab, James Younger
(Yale University Press, 1999)

The Solar System
Michael A. Seeds
(Brooks Cole, 2007)

Universe
Roger Freedman), William J. Kaufmann
(W. H. Freeman, 2007)

Universe: The Definitive Visual Guide
(Dorling Kindersley, 2005)

INDEX

ACKNOWLEDGMENTS

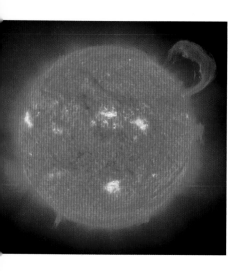

AUTHOR ACKNOWLEDGMENTS

I am grateful to veteran astronomy authors Ian Ridpath and Robin Scagell for their encouragement and advice when I undertook this exciting and enjoyable project, and to the team at Ivy Press who have produced such an attractive design. In particular, I must thank my editor, Simon Smith, who made sure that I kept on track and Greg Smye-Rumsby for his spectacular and powerful artwork.

PICTURE CREDITS

The publisher would like to thank the following individuals and organizations for their kind permission to reproduce the images in this book. Every effort has been made to acknowledge the pictures, however we apologize if there are any unintentional omissions. **akg-images** 17; 32t; 35 center; 42tl; 113tl; /Joseph Martin: 130; /Erich Lessing: 136tl; 150tl. **Anthony Ayiomamitis** 48tr, 50tl. **T. Beers**, after John Polgreen: 64. **The Bridgeman Art Library** 9; 68; /Collection Kharbine-Tapabor, Paris, France: 75b; /Vatican Museums and Galleries, Vatican City, Italy: 89tr; /National Maritime Museum, London: 106; 150br; /Marcel Lecomte Collection, Paris, France, Giraudon: 152tl; /© Christie's Images: 152bl. **Center for Space Physics, Boston University** 56, 59tr. **Lorenzo Comolli** 62. **Ben Cooper** 121. **Corbis** /© Bryan Allen: 147. **Sebastian Deiries (ESO)** 135. **ESA** 59b; 63br; /DLR/FU Berlin (G. Neukum): 78 t and bl; /DLR/FU Berlin (G. Neukum) MOC Malin Space Science Systems: 81bl; 100 center. **ESO** 144bl. **David Graham** 55t, 153tr. **Nick Howes** 107bl. **The International Astronomical Union** /Martin Kornmesser: 21tr. **iStock** /Sergii Tsololo: 1; /George Argyropoulos: 2–3; /Thomas Tuchan: outer gatefold. **Jupiter Images** 13, 14tl, 16, 31, 49tr, 74. **Yoko Kikuta** 40b. **Laurent Laveder/www.pixheaven.net** 41br. **Lowell Observatory Archives** 118bl. **LP Pics** 80tl, 119. **Mary Evans Picture Library** 27, 107bl, 111tr, 112b. 126bl, 138tl. **Massachusetts Institute of Technology Kavli Institute for Astrophysics and Space Research** 65. **Master and Fellows of Trinity College Cambridge** 86. **Meade Instruments Corporation** 151. **NASA** 19, 24, 108tr, 113tr 115t, 123tr, 126tl, 126br, 127; /G. Bacon (STScI): 122; /James Bell (Cornell Univ.), Michael Wolff (Space Science Institute) and The Hubble Heritage Team (STScI/AURA): 77tr; 78tr; /J. Clarke (University of Michigan): 93b; /ESA, D.R. Ardila (JHU), D.A. Golimowski (JHU), J.E. Krist (STScI/JPL), M. Clampin (NASA/GSFC), J.P. Williams (UH/IfA), J.P. Blakeslee (JHU), H.C. Ford (JHU), G.F. Hartig (STScI), G.D. Illingworth (UCO-Lick) and the ACS Science Team: 18; /ESA, D. Golimowski (Johns Hopkins University), D. Ardila (IPAC), J. Krist (JPL), M. Clampin (GSFC), H. Ford (JHU), and G. Illingworth (UCO/Lick) and the ACS Science Team: 144br; /ESA/D.Hines(SSI)/G.Schneider (University of Arizona): 145; /ESA, IRTF, and A. Sánchez-Lavega and R. Hueso (Universidad del País Vasco, Spain): 88br; /ESA, H. Weaver (JHU/APL), A. Stern (SwRI), and the HST Pluto Companion Search Team: 120tl; /GSFC/METI/ERSDAC/JAROS, and U.S./Japan ASTER Science Team: 128bl; /ISS: 137; /JPL: 41tr, 42bl, 43, 44 center, 45b, 46b, 47bl, 47t, 58l, 58r, 73r, 76, 77b, 82b, 83tr, 88tl, 89b, 92, 108tl, 110b, 111b, 114t, 120 center, 123br, 134tl; /JPL/Arizona State University/Ron Miller: 79br; /JPL-Caltech: 142; /JPL-Caltech/R. Hurt (SSC): 143bl; /JPL-Caltech/University of Arizona: 81r, 82t, 83 center; /JPL-Caltech/University of Arizona/Cornell/Ohio State University: 79tl, 79tr; /JPL/DLR: 91; /JPL/ESA/University of Arizona:100 t and bl; /JPL/MSSS: 75tl; /JPL/Space Science Institute: 96, 98, 101b, 102, 103; /JPL/STScI: 109br; /JPL/University of Arizona: 99; /JPL/USGS: 101tr; /JSC: 131br; /Erich Karkoschka (University of Arizona Lunar & Planetary Lab): 109tr; /KSC: 51, 57; /NSSDC: 44tl; /NSSCD/GSFS: 63tr, 90l; /SOHO/NASA/ESA: 26tl, 34, 36, 37b, 160 /Tunc Tezel: 15; /Eliot Young (SwRI) et al.: 118tl. **Optical Mechanics Inc:** 143r. **Jurgen Schmoll** 7, 48tl. **Science Photo Library** /Eckhard Slawik: 12 center; 25; 46tl; /Royal Astronomical Society: 69; /NASA: 80bl; /NASA: 83br; /NASA: 90r, 114br; /MSSO, ANU: 93tr; 97tl; 107tl; 112tl; /David A. Hardy, Futures: 50 Years in Space: 115br; /Mark Garlick: 128tr; /Ria Novosti: 129; 138 center. **Greg Smye-Rumsby** 6, 11, 14 center, 23, 26br, 29, 30; 35t, center, br; 39, 42 center, 49br, 50b, 53, 55b, 61, 71, 72, 85, 87, 95, 105, 110l, 117, 125, 131tr, 133, 134tr, 141. **Snr Airman Joshua Strang/UASF/Air Force Link** 37tr. **Paul Sutherland** 40tl, 45tr, 48bl, 54, 66, 67l, 73l, 136br, 139. **Paul Sutherland/Anthony Ayiomamitis** 33. **Paul Sutherland/Yoko Kikuta** 32b. **Dave Tyler** 67r, 153bl **University of Virginia Department of Astronomy** 75tr.